A MIDSUMMER NIGHT'S DREAM

William Shakespeare

Prestwick House

LITERARY TOUCHSTONE CLASSICS™

P.O. Box 658 Clayton, Delaware 19938 • www.prestwickhouse.com

This book is dedicated to the memory of
Paul Arrington
our colleague and friend.

SENIOR EDITOR: Paul Moliken

COVER ILLUSTRATION: Larry Knox
Costumes provided by www.actorsattic.com

PRODUCTION: Chris Koniencki

PRESTWICK HOUSE
LITERARY TOUCHSTONE CLASSICS

P.O. BOX 658
CLAYTON, DELAWARE 19938
TEL: 1.800.932.4593
FAX: 1.888.718.9333
WEB: www.prestwickhouse.com

ISBN   978-1-58049-588-2

CONTENTS

STRATEGIES

Strategies for Understanding Shakespeare's Language

1. When reading verse, note the appropriate phrasing and intonation.

    DO NOT PAUSE AT THE END OF A LINE unless there is a mark of punctuation. Shakespearean verse has a rhythm of its own, and once a reader gets used to it, the rhythm becomes very natural to speak in and read. Beginning readers often find it helpful to read a short pause at a comma and a long pause for a period, colon, semicolon, dash, or question mark. Here's an example from *The Merchant of Venice*, Act IV, Scene i:

    > The quality of mercy is not strain'd, (*short pause*)
    > It droppeth as the gentle rain from heaven
    > Upon the place beneath: (*long pause*) it is twice blest; (*long pause*)
    > It blesseth him that gives, (*short pause*) and him that takes; (*long pause*)
    > 'Tis mightiest in the mighties; (*long pause*) it becomes
    > The throned monarch better than his crown; (*long pause*)

2. Read from punctuation mark to punctuation mark for meaning.

    In addition to helping you read aloud, punctuation marks define units of thought. Try to understand each unit as you read, keeping in mind that periods, colons, semicolons, and question marks signal the end of a thought. Here's an example from *The Taming of the Shrew*, Act I, Scene i:

    > Luc. Tranio, I saw her coral lips to move,
    >   And with her breath she did perfume the air;
    >   Sacred, and sweet, was all I saw in her.
    > Tra. Nay, then, 'tis time to stir him from his trance.
    >   I pray, awake, sir: if you love the maid,
    >   Bend thoughts and wits to achieve her.

The first unit of thought is from "Tranio" to "air":
He saw her lips move, and her breath perfumed the air.

The second thought ("Sacred, and sweet...") re-emphasizes the first.

Tranio replies that Lucentio needs to awaken from his trance and try
to win "the maid." These two sentences can be considered one unit of
thought.

3. In an **inverted sentence**, the verb comes before the subject. Some lines will
    be easier to understand if you put the subject first and reword the sentence.
    For example, look at the line below:

    "*Never was seen so black a day as this:*" (*Romeo and Juliet*, Act IV, Scene v)

    You can change its inverted pattern so it is more easily understood:

    "*A day as black as this was never seen:*"

4. An **ellipsis** occurs when a word or phrase is left out. In *Romeo and Juliet*,
    Benvolio asks Romeo's father and mother if they know the problem that is
    bothering their son. Romeo's father answers:

    "*I neither know **it** nor can learn of **him***" (*Romeo and Juliet*, Act I, Scene i)

    This sentence can easily be understood to mean,

    "*I neither know [the cause of] it,
    nor can [I] learn [about it from] him.*"

5. As you read longer speeches, keep track of the subject, verb, and object—
    who did what to whom.

    In the clauses below, note the subject, verbs, and objects:

    Ross: The king hath happily received, Macbeth,
        The news of thy success: and when he reads
        Thy personal venture in the rebel's fight... (*Macbeth*, Act I, Scene iii)

    1ˢᵗ clause: *The king hath happily received, Macbeth,/The news of thy success:*
    SUBJECT – The king
    VERB – has received
    OBJECT – the news [of Macbeth's success]

2nd clause: *and when he reads/thy personal venture in the rebel's fight,*
SUBJECT – he [the king]
VERB – reads
OBJECT – [about] your venture

In addition to following the subject, verb, and object of a clause, you also need to track pronoun references. In the following soliloquy, Romeo, who is madly in love with Juliet, secretly observes her as she steps out on her balcony. To help you keep track of the pronoun references, we've made margin notes. (Note that the feminine pronoun sometimes refers to Juliet, but sometimes does not.)

> But, soft! what light through yonder window breaks?
> It is the east, and Juliet is the sun!
> Arise, fair sun, and kill the envious moon,
> Who* is already sick and pale with grief,   *"Who" refers to the moon.*
> That thou her* maid* art more fair than she:*   *"thou her maid" refers to Juliet, the sun.*
>   *"she" and "her" refer to the moon.*

In tracking the line of action in a passage, it is useful to identify the main thoughts that are being expressed and paraphrase them. Note the following passage in which Hamlet expresses his feelings about the death of his father and the remarriage of his mother:

> O God! a beast that wants discourse of reason
> Would have mourn'd longer—married with my uncle,
> My father's brother, but no more like my father
> Than I to Hercules. (*Hamlet*, Act I, Scene ii)

Paraphrasing the three main points, we find that Hamlet is saying:

- a mindless beast would have mourned the death of its mate longer than my mother did
- she married my uncle, my father's brother
- my uncle is not at all like my father

If you are having trouble understanding Shakespeare, the first rule is to read it out loud, just as an actor rehearsing would have to do. That will help you understand how one thought is connected to another.

6.   Shakespeare frequently uses **metaphor** to illustrate an idea in a unique way. Pay careful attention to the two dissimilar objects or ideas being compared.

In *Macbeth*, Duncan, the king says:

> I have begun to plant thee, and will labour
> To make thee full of growing. (*Macbeth*, Act I, Scene v)

The king compares Macbeth to a tree he can plant and watch grow.

7. An **allusion** is a reference to some event, person, place, or artistic work, not directly explained or discussed by the writer; it relies on the reader's familiarity with the item referred to. Allusion is a quick way of conveying information or presenting an image. In the following lines, Romeo alludes to Diana, goddess of the hunt and of chastity, and to Cupid's arrow (love).

> ROMEO: Well, in that hit you miss: she'll not be hit
> with Cupid's arrow, she hath Dian's wit;
> and in strong proof of chastity well arm'd
> (*Romeo and Juliet*, Act I, Scene i)

8. Contracted words are words in which a letter has been left out. Some that frequently appear:

be't	on't	wi'	do't
t'	'sblood	'gainst	ta'en
i'	'tis	e'en	'bout
know'st	'twill	ne'er	o'
o'er			

9. Archaic, obsolete, and familiar words with unfamiliar definitions may also cause problems.

-   **Archaic Words:** Some archaic words, like *thee, thou, thy,* and *thine,* are instantly understandable, while others, like *betwixt,* cause a momentary pause.

-   **Obsolete Words:** If it were not for the notes in a Shakespeare text, obsolete words could be a problem; words like *beteem* are usually not found in student dictionaries. In these situations, however, a quick glance at the book's notes will solve the problem.

-   **Familiar Words with Unfamiliar Definitions:** Another problem is those familiar words whose definitions have changed. Because readers think they know the word, they do not check the notes. For example, in this comment from *Much Ado About Nothing,* Act I, Scene i, the word *an* means "if":

BEATRICE: Scratching could not make it worse, *an* 'twere such
            a face as yours were.

For this kind of word, we have included margin notes.

10. Wordplay—puns, double entendres, and malapropisms:

- A **pun** is a literary device that achieves humor or emphasis by playing on ambiguities. Two distinct meanings are suggested either by the same word or by two similar-sounding words.

- A **double entendre** is a kind of pun in which a word or phrase has a second, usually sexual, meaning.

- A **malapropism** occurs when a character mistakenly uses a word that he or she has confused with another word. In *Romeo and Juliet*, the Nurse tells Romeo that she needs to have a "confidence" with him, when she should have said "conference." Mockingly, Benvolio then says she probably will "indite" (rather than "invite") Romeo to dinner.

11. Shakespeare's Language:

Our final word on Shakespeare's language is adapted by special permission from Ralph Alan Cohen's book *Shakesfear and How to Cure It—A Guide to Teaching Shakespeare*.

What's so hard about Shakespeare's language? Many students come to Shakespeare's language assuming that the language of his period is substantially different from ours. In fact, 98% of the words in Shakespeare are current-usage English words. So why does it sometimes seem hard to read Shakespeare? There are three main reasons:

- Originally, Shakespeare wrote the words for an actor to illustrate them as he spoke. In short, the play you have at hand was meant for the stage, not for the page.

- Shakespeare had the same love of reforming and rearranging words in such places as hip-hop and sportscasting today. His plays reflect an excitement about language and an inventiveness that becomes enjoyable once the reader gets into the spirit of it.

- Since Shakespeare puts all types of people on stage, those characters will include some who are pompous, some who are devious, some who are boring, and some who are crazy, and all of these will speak in ways that are sometimes trying. Modern playwrights creating similar characters have them speak in similarly challenging ways.

12. Stage Directions:

Shakespeare's stagecraft went hand-in-hand with his wordcraft. For that reason, we believe it is important for the reader to know which stage directions are modern and which derive from Shakespeare's earliest text—the single-play Quartos or the Folio, the first collected works (1623). All stage directions appear in italics, but the brackets enclose modern additions to the stage directions. Readers may assume that the unbracketed stage directions appear in the Quarto and/or Folio versions of the play.

13. Scene Locations:

Shakespeare imagined his plays, first and foremost, on the stage of his outdoor or indoor theatre. The original printed versions of the plays do not give imaginary scene locations, except when they are occasionally mentioned in the dialogue. As an aid to the reader, this edition does include scene locations at the beginning of each scene, but puts all such locations in brackets to remind the reader that *this is not what Shakespeare envisioned and only possibly what he imagined.*

Reading Pointers for Sharper Insights

Readers should look for incidents or comments that support these major concepts in the play:

1. The relationship between reality and fantasy:

    A Midsummer Night's Dream explores several levels of consciousness and awareness. Dreams, altered states, and the presence of mythical creatures distort reality for some of the characters. As you progress through the play, pay attention to how the mixing of these worlds confuses the characters and adds humor.

2. The various types of love:

    The love among couples in this play varies by type, degree, and source. Take note of how love changes throughout the course of *A Midsummer Night's Dream*.

3. The balance between the rational and the irrational, and the necessity of both forces:

    In this play, science and reason (the rational), are at odds with love and magic (the irrational). Pay special attention to the sources of conflicts in the play, and also notice which one of the opposing forces seems to provide resolution to the problems. In the play, logic and social custom comprise the rational. Art, magic, myth, and action based on emotion comprise the irrational.

As you read, be aware of the following elements and terms, and note when each appears:

- allusion
- malapropism
- pun
- double entendre
- The opposition motif: Identify the contrasting pairs of characters and the elements of setting. In many instances, these pairs are complete opposites; for example, night and day, love and hate, beauty and ugliness, the city and the country, grace and foolishness, etc..
- Styles of speech determined by characters' social status or emotional state: Watch for changes in rhyme and meter, and note which character is speaking when a change occurs.

A Midsummer Night's Dream

William Shakespeare

DRAMATIS PERSONAE

THESEUS, Duke of Athens
HIPPOLYTA, Queen of the Amazons, bethrothed to Theseus
PHILOSTRATE, Master of the Revels to Theseus
EGEUS, father to Hermia
LYSANDER, in love with Hermia
DEMETRIUS, in love with Hermia
HERMIA, daughter to Egeus, in love with Lysander
HELENA, in love with Demetrius

OBERON, King of the Fairies
TITANIA, Queen of the Fairies
PUCK, or ROBIN GOODFELLOW
PEASEBLOSSOM, fairy
COBWEB, fairy
MOTH, fairy
MUSTARDSEED, fairy

QUINCE, a carpenter
SNUG, a joiner
BOTTOM, a weaver
FLUTE, a bellows-mender
SNOUT, a tinker
STARVELING, a tailor

PROLOGUE, PYRAMUS, THISBE, WALL, MOONSHINE, LION are presented
by: QUINCE, BOTTOM, FLUTE, SNOUT, STARVELING, AND SNUG

Other Fairies attending their King and Queen
Attendants on Theseus and Hippolyta

ACT I

SCENE I
[The Palace of Theseus in Athens]

Enter Theseus, Hippolyta, [with Philostrate, and Attendants]

THESEUS: Now, fair Hippolyta, our nuptial hour
    Draws on apace;[1] four happy days bring in
    Another moon; but, O, methinks, how slow
    This old moon wanes![2] She lingers[3] my desires,
5   Like to a step-dame[4] or a dowager,[5]†
    Long withering out a young man's revenue.[6]
HIPPOLYTA: Four days will quickly steep[7] themselves in night;
    Four nights will quickly dream away the time;†
    And then the moon, like to a silver bow
10   New-bent in heaven, shall behold the night
    Of our solemnities.[8]
THESEUS: Go, Philostrate,
    Stir up the Athenian youth to merriments;
    Awake the pert[9] and nimble spirit of mirth;
15   Turn melancholy forth to funerals;
    The pale companion is not for our pomp.[10]
                       [Exit Philostrate]
    Hippolyta, I woo'd thee with my sword,
    And won thy love doing thee injuries;
    But I will wed thee in another key,
20   With pomp, with triumph, and with revelling.

Enter Egeus, and his daughter Hermia, Lysander, and Demetrius

EGEUS: Happy be Theseus, our renowned duke!
THESEUS: Thanks, good Egeus; what's the news with thee?

[1] *quickly*

[2] *goes down, vanishes*

[3] *delays*

[4] *stepmother*

[5] *widow*

[6] *inheritance*

[7] *plunge*

[8] *marriage festivities*

[9] *lively*

[10] *ceremony*

†Terms marked in the text with (†) can be looked up in the Glossary for additional information.

[11]*agitation*

EGEUS: Full of vexation[11] come I, with complaint
Against my child, my daughter Hermia.
25   Stand forth, Demetrius. My noble lord,
This man hath my consent to marry her.
Stand forth, Lysander. And, my gracious duke,
This man hath bewitch'd the bosom of my child.
Thou, thou, Lysander, thou hast given her rhymes,
30   And interchanged love-tokens with my child;
Thou hast by moonlight at her window sung,

[12]*insincere*

With feigning[12] voice, verses of feigning love,

[13]*trinkets*

And stolen the impression of her fantasy

[14]*fancy gifts*

With bracelets of thy hair, rings, gawds,[13] conceits,[14]
35   Knacks, trifles, nosegays,[15] sweetmeats, messengers

[15]*showy flowers*

Of strong prevailment[16] in unharden'd youth;

[16]*persuasiveness*

With cunning hast thou filch'd[17] my daughter's heart;

[17]*stolen*

Turn'd her obedience, which is due to me,
To stubborn harshness. And, my gracious duke,
40   Be it so she will not here before your Grace†
Consent to marry with Demetrius,
I beg the ancient privilege of Athens:
As she is mine, I may dispose of her;†
Which shall be either to this gentleman

[18]*Clearly*

45   Or to her death, according to our law
Immediately[18] provided in that case.
THESEUS: What say you, Hermia? Be advis'd, fair maid.
To you your father should be as a god;
One that composed your beauties; yea, and one
50   To whom you are but as a form in wax,
By him imprinted, and within his power
To leave the figure, or disfigure it.
Demetrius is a worthy gentleman.
HERMIA: So is Lysander.
55 THESEUS: In himself he is;

[19]*case, situation*

But in this kind,[19] wanting your father's voice,
The other must be held the worthier.
HERMIA: I would my father look'd but with my eyes.
THESEUS: Rather your eyes must with his judgment look.
60 HERMIA: I do entreat your Grace to pardon me.
I know not by what power I am made bold,
Nor how it may concern my modesty,

In such a presence here to plead my thoughts;
But I beseech your Grace that I may know
65   The worst that may befall me in this case,
If I refuse to wed Demetrius.
THESEUS: Either to die the death, or to abjure
For ever the society of men.
Therefore, fair Hermia, question your desires,
70   Know of your youth, examine well your blood,
Whether, if you yield not to your father's choice,
You can endure the livery[20] of a nun,
For aye[21] to be in shady cloister[22] mew'd,[23]
To live a barren sister all your life,
75   Chanting faint hymns to the cold fruitless moon.†
Thrice-blessed they that master so their blood
To undergo such maiden pilgrimage;†
But earthlier happy is the rose distill'd[24]
Than that which, withering on the virgin thorn
80   Grows, lives, and dies, in single blessedness.
HERMIA: So will I grow, so live, so die, my lord,
Ere I will yield my virgin patent[25] up
Unto his lordship, whose unwished yoke[26]
My soul consents not to give sovereignty.[27]
85 THESEUS: Take time to pause; and by the next new moon—
The sealing-day betwixt my love and me
For everlasting bond of fellowship,—
Upon that day either prepare to die
For disobedience to your father's will,
90   Or else to wed Demetrius, as he would,
Or on Diana's† altar to protest[28]
For aye[29] austerity[30] and single life.
DEMETRIUS: Relent, sweet Hermia; and, Lysander, yield
Thy crazed title to my certain right.
95 LYSANDER: You have her father's love, Demetrius;
Let me have Hermia's; do you marry him.
EGEUS: Scornful Lysander! True, he hath my love;
And what is mine my love shall render him;
And she is mine; and all my right of her
100   I do estate unto Demetrius.
LYSANDER: I am, my lord, as well derived as he,
As well possess'd; my love is more than his;

[20]*clothing; uniform*

[21]*forever*

[22] *a convent, monastery*

[23]*caged*

[24]*processed into perfume*

[25]*the right to remain a virgin*

[26]*restraint*

[27]*power*

[28]*vow*

[29]*ever, always*

[30]*childless*

        My fortunes every way as fairly rank'd,

[31]*even more*   If not with vantage,[31] as Demetrius';

105   And, which is more than all these boasts can be,

        I am belov'd of beauteous Hermia.

        Why should not I then prosecute my right?

        Demetrius, I'll avouch it to his head,

[32]*courted, dated*   Made love to[32] Nedar's daughter, Helena,

110   And won her soul; and she, sweet lady, dotes,

        Devoutly dotes, dotes in idolatry,

        Upon this spotted† and inconstant man.

    THESEUS: I must confess that I have heard so much,

        And with Demetrius thought to have spoke thereof;

115   But, being over-full of self-affairs,

        My mind did lose it. But, Demetrius, come;

        And come, Egeus; you shall go with me;

[33]*advice*   I have some private schooling[33] for you both.

[34]*prepare*   For you, fair Hermia, look you arm[34] yourself

120   To fit your fancies to your father's will,

        Or else the law of Athens yields you up—

[35]*lessen; change*   Which by no means we may extenuate[35]—

        To death, or to a vow of single life.

        Come, my Hippolyta; what cheer, my love?

125   Demetrius and Egeus, go along;

        I must employ you in some business

[36]*in preparation of* Against[36] our nuptial, and confer with you

        Of something nearly that concerns yourselves.

    EGEUS: With duty and desire we follow you.

               Exeunt [all but] Lysander and Hermia

130 LYSANDER: How now, my love! Why is your cheek so pale?

        How chance the roses there do fade so fast?

[37]*probably*   HERMIA: Belike[37] for want[38] of rain, which I could well

[38]*lack*   Beteem[39] them from the tempest[40] of my eyes.

    LYSANDER: Ay me! for aught that I could ever read,

[39]*give* 135   Could ever hear by tale or history,

        The course of true love never did run smooth;

[40]*storm*   But, either it was different in blood[41]—

[41]*breeding, class* HERMIA: O cross![42] too high to be enthrall'd to low.

[42]*bother, irritation* LYSANDER: Or else misgraffed[43] in respect of years—

[43]*mismatched* 140 HERMIA: O spite! too old to be engag'd to young.

    LYSANDER: Or else it stood upon the choice of friends—

HERMIA: O hell! to choose love by another's eyes.
LYSANDER: Or, if there were a sympathy[44] in choice,
    War, death, or sickness, did lay siege to it,
145   Making it momentany[45] as a sound,
    Swift as a shadow, short as any dream,
    Brief as the lightning in the collied[46] night
    That, in a spleen,[47] unfolds[48] both heaven and earth,
    And ere[49] a man hath power to say 'Behold!'
150   The jaws of darkness do devour it up;
    So quick bright things come to confusion.
HERMIA: If then true lovers have been ever cross'd,
    It stands as an edict in destiny.
    Then let us teach our trial patience,[50]
155   Because it is a customary cross,
    As due to love as thoughts and dreams and sighs,
    Wishes and tears, poor fancy's[51] followers.
LYSANDER: A good persuasion; therefore, hear me, Hermia.
    I have a widow aunt, a dowager
160   Of great revenue, and she hath no child:
    From Athens is her house remote seven leagues;[†]
    And she respects[52] me as her only son.
    There, gentle Hermia, may I marry thee;
    And to that place the sharp Athenian law
165   Cannot pursue us. If thou lovest me then,
    Steal forth[53] thy father's house tomorrow night;
    And in the wood, a league without the town,
    Where I did meet thee once with Helena
    To do observance to a morn of May,[†]
170   There will I stay for thee.
HERMIA: My good Lysander!
    I swear to thee, by Cupid's strongest bow,
    By his best arrow, with the golden head,[†]
    By the simplicity[54] of Venus' doves,[†]
175   By that which knitteth[55] souls and prospers loves,
    And by that fire which burn'd the Carthage Queen,
    When the false Trojan under sail was seen,[†]
    By all the vows that ever men have broke,
    In number more than ever women spoke,
180   In that same place thou hast appointed me,
    Tomorrow truly will I meet with thee.

[44]*agreement*

[45]*momentary*

[46]*coal-black*

[47]*fury*

[48]*reveals*

[49]*before*

[50]*"Allow us to be taught patience during this trial…"*

[51]*love's*

[52]*regards*

[53]*"Sneak away from…"*

[54]*innocence*

[55]*binds*

LYSANDER: Keep promise, love. Look, here comes Helena.

Enter Helena

HERMIA: God speed fair Helena! Whither away?[56]

HELENA: Call you me fair? That fair again unsay.
185 Demetrius loves your fair. O happy fair![57]
 Your eyes are lode-stars[58] and your tongue's sweet air
 More tuneable than lark to shepherd's ear,
 When wheat is green, when hawthorn buds appear.
 Sickness is catching; O, were favor so,
190 Yours would I catch, fair Hermia, ere I go!
 My ear should catch your voice, my eye your eye,
 My tongue should catch your tongue's sweet melody.
 Were the world mine, Demetrius being bated,[59]
 The rest I'd give to be to you translated.[60]
195 O, teach me how you look, and with what art
 You sway the motion of Demetrius' heart!

HERMIA: I frown upon him, yet he loves me still.

HELENA: O that your frowns would teach my smiles such
 skill!

200 HERMIA: I give him curses, yet he gives me love.

HELENA: O that my prayers could such affection move!

HERMIA: The more I hate, the more he follows me.

HELENA: The more I love, the more he hateth me.

HERMIA: His folly, Helena, is no fault of mine.

205 HELENA: None, but your beauty; would that fault were
 mine!

HERMIA: Take comfort: he no more shall see my face;
 Lysander and myself will fly this place.
 Before the time I did Lysander see,
210 Seem'd Athens as a paradise to me.
 O, then, what graces in my love do dwell,
 That he hath turn'd a heaven unto a hell!

LYSANDER: Helen, to you our minds we will unfold:
 Tomorrow night, when Phoebe† doth behold
215 Her silver visage in the watery glass,
 Decking with liquid pearl the bladed grass,
 A time that lovers' flights doth still conceal,
 Through Athens' gates have we devised to steal.

HERMIA: And in the wood, where often you and I

---

[56]*"To what place are you going?"*

[57]*beauty*

[58]*guiding stars*

[59]*excepted*

[60]*transformed*

220 Upon faint primrose-beds were wont[61] to lie,
   Emptying our bosoms of their counsel[62] sweet,
   There my Lysander and myself shall meet;
   And thence from Athens turn away our eyes,
   To seek new friends and stranger companies.
225 Farewell, sweet playfellow; pray thou for us,
   And good luck grant thee thy Demetrius!
   Keep word, Lysander; we must starve our sight
   From lovers' food till morrow deep midnight. *Exit Hermia*
  LYSANDER: I will, my Hermia. Helena, adieu;
230 As you on him, Demetrius dote on you.

             Exit Lysander

  HELENA: How happy some o'er other some† can be!
   Through Athens I am thought as fair as she.
   But what of that? Demetrius thinks not so;
   He will not know what all but he do know.
235 And as he errs,[63] doting on Hermia's eyes,
   So I, admiring of his qualities.
   Things base and vile, holding no quantity,[64]
   Love can transpose[65] to form and dignity.
   Love looks not with the eyes, but with the mind;
240 And therefore is wing'd Cupid painted blind.
   Nor hath Love's mind of any judgment taste;
   Wings and no eyes, figure[66] unheedy haste;
   And therefore is Love said to be a child,
   Because in choice he is so oft beguiled.[67]
245 As waggish[68] boys in game themselves forswear,[69]
   So the boy Love is perjured everywhere;
   For ere Demetrius look'd on Hermia's eyne,[70]
   He hail'd[71] down oaths that he was only mine;
   And when this hail some heat from Hermia felt,
250 So he dissolv'd, and showers of oaths did melt.
   I will go tell him of fair Hermia's flight;
   Then to the wood will he tomorrow night
   Pursue her; and for this intelligence[72]
   If I have thanks, it is a dear expense.
255 But herein[73] mean I to enrich my pain,
   To have his sight thither[74] and back again.

           Exit

---

[61]accustomed

[62]innermost thoughts

[63]goes astray

[64]proportion, shape

[65]change

[66]symbolize

[67]tricked, cheated

[68]playful

[69]swear falsely, deny

[70]eyes

[71]showered

[72]information

[73]in this

[74]there

SCENE II
[Athens]

*Enter Quince[†] the Carpenter, Snug[†] the Joiner, Bottom[†] the Weaver,
Flute the Bellows-mender, Snout the Tinker, and Starveling[†] the
Taylor*

QUINCE: Is all our company here?

BOTTOM: You were best to call them generally,[1†] man by
man, according to the scrip.[2]

QUINCE: Here is the scroll of every man's name, which is
5   thought fit, through all Athens, to play in our interlude
before the duke and the duchess on his wedding-day at
night.

BOTTOM: First, good Peter Quince, say what the play treats
on;[3] then read the names of the actors; and so grow to a
10   point.[4]

QUINCE: Marry, our play is, *The Most Lamentable Comedy
and Most Cruel Death of Pyramus and Thisbe.*

BOTTOM: A very good piece of work, I assure you, and a
merry.[5] Now, good Peter Quince, call forth your actors
15   by the scroll. Masters, spread yourselves.

QUINCE: Answer as I call you. Nick Bottom, the weaver.

BOTTOM: Ready. Name what part I am for, and proceed.

QUINCE: You, Nick Bottom, are set down for Pyramus.

BOTTOM: What is Pyramus? A lover, or a tyrant?

20 QUINCE: A lover, that kills himself most gallant for love.

BOTTOM: That will ask some tears in the true performing
of it. If I do it, let the audience look to their eyes; I will
move storms; I will condole[6] in some measure. To the
rest: yet my chief humor[7] is for a tyrant. I could play
25   Ercles[8] rarely,[9] or a part to tear a cat[10] in, to make all
split.[11]

> 'The raging rocks
> And shivering shocks
> Shall break the locks
> 30   Of prison gates;
> And Phibbus'[†] car[12]
> Shall shine from far,

---

[1] *"individually"*

[2] *list*

[3] *deals with*

[4] *come to a conclusion*

[5] *comedy*

[6] *mourn*

[7] *tendency, aim*

[8] *Hercules*

[9] *well*

[10] *rant, rave*

[11] *burst with emotion*

[12] *chariot*

        And make and mar
          The foolish Fates.'†

35   This was lofty! Now name the rest of the players. This is
      Ercles' vein,[13] a tyrant's vein: a lover is more condoling.

      QUINCE: Francis Flute, the bellows-mender.

      FLUTE: Here, Peter Quince.

      QUINCE: Flute, you must take Thisbe on you.

40 FLUTE: What is Thisbe? A wandering knight?

      QUINCE: It is the lady that Pyramus must love.

      FLUTE: Nay, faith, let not me play a woman; I have a beard
        coming.†

      QUINCE: That's all one; you shall play it in a mask, and you
45   may speak as small[14] as you will.

      BOTTOM: An[15] I may hide my face, let me play Thisbe too. I'll
        speak in a monstrous little voice: 'Thisne, Thisne!' *[Then
        speaking small]* 'Ah Pyramus, my lover dear! Thy Thisbe
        dear, and lady dear!'

50 QUINCE: No, no, you must play Pyramus; and, Flute, you
        Thisbe.

      BOTTOM: Well, proceed.

      QUINCE: Robin Starveling, the tailor.

      STARVELING: Here, Peter Quince.

55 QUINCE: Robin Starveling, you must play Thisbe's mother.
        Tom Snout, the tinker.

      SNOUT: Here, Peter Quince.

      QUINCE: You, Pyramus' father; myself, Thisbe's father; Snug,
        the joiner, you, the lion's part. And, I hope, here is a play
60   fitted.[16]

      SNUG: Have you the lion's part written? Pray you,[17] if it be,
        give it me, for I am slow of study.

      QUINCE: You may do it extempore,[18] for it is nothing but
        roaring.

65 BOTTOM: Let me play the lion too. I will roar that I will do
        any man's heart good to hear me; I will roar, that I will
        make the duke say 'Let him roar again, let him roar again.'

      QUINCE: An you should do it too terribly, you would fright
        the duchess and the ladies, that they would shriek; and
70   that were enough to hang us all.

      ALL: That would hang us, every mother's son.

      BOTTOM: I grant you, friends, if you should fright the ladies

[13]*attitude*

[14]*high-pitched*

[15]*If*

[16]*well cast*

[17]*Please*

[18]*with little or no preparation (extemporaneously)*

[19]*"moderate"*

[20]*"sitting dove" and "sucking lamb"*

[21]*as though it were*

[22]*handsome*

[23]*dark red*

[24]*gold*

[25]*memorize*

[26]*plans*

[27]*list of stage props*

out of their wits, they would have no more discretion but to hang us; but I will aggravate[19] my voice so, that I

75   will roar you as gently as any sucking dove;[20] I will roar you an't were[21] any nightingale.

QUINCE: You can play no part but Pyramus; for Pyramus is a sweet-faced man; a proper[22] man, as one shall see in a summer's day; a most lovely gentleman-like man; there-

80   fore you must needs play Pyramus.

BOTTOM: Well, I will undertake it. What beard were I best to play it in?

QUINCE: Why, what you will.

BOTTOM: I will discharge it in either your straw color beard,

85   your orange-tawny beard, your purple-in-grain[23] beard, or your French crown[24] color beard, your perfect yellow.

QUINCE: Some of your French crowns have no hair at all,† and then you will play barefaced. But, masters, here are your parts; and I am to entreat you, request you, and

90   desire you, to con[25] them by tomorrow night; and meet me in the palace wood, a mile without the town, by moonlight; there will we rehearse; for if we meet in the city, we shall be dogg'd with company, and our devices[26] known. In the meantime I will draw a bill of proper-

95   ties,[27] such as our play wants. I pray you, fail me not.

BOTTOM: We will meet; and there we may rehearse most obscenely and courageously. Take pains; be perfect; adieu.

QUINCE: At the duke's oak we meet.

100   BOTTOM: Enough; hold, or cut bow-strings.†

Exeunt

ACT II

SCENE I
[A wood near Athens]

Enter a Fairy at one door, and Robin Goodfellow [Puck†]
at another.]

PUCK: How now, spirit! whither wander you?
FAIRY: Over hill, over dale,
    Thorough[1] bush, thorough brier,
  Over park, over pale,[2]
5   Thorough flood, thorough fire,
  I do wander every where,
  Swifter than the moon's sphere;†
  And I serve the fairy queen,
  To dew her orbs[3] upon the green.
10 The cowslips[4] tall her pensioners[5] be;
  In their gold coats spots you see;
  Those be rubies, fairy favors,[6]
  In those freckles live their savors.[7]
  I must go seek some dewdrops here,
15 And hang a pearl in every cowslip's ear.
  Farewell, thou lob[8] of spirits; I'll be gone.
  Our queen and all her elves come here anon.[9]
PUCK: The king doth keep his revels[10] here tonight;
  Take heed the queen come not within his sight;
20 For Oberon is passing fell[11] and wrath,
  Because that she as her attendant hath
  A lovely boy, stolen from an Indian king.
  She never had so sweet a changeling;†
  And jealous Oberon would have the child
25 Knight of his train, to trace the forests wild;
  But she perforce[12] withholds the loved boy,

[1]*through*

[2]*fenced land*

[3]*sprinkle fairy rings*

[4]*wildflowers*

[5]*royal bodyguards*

[6]*gifts*

[7]*scents*

[8]*oaf, bumpkin*

[9]*soon*

[10]*entertainment*

[11]*cruel*

[12]*forcibly*

[13]spring

[14]shining

[15]quarrel

[16]physical appear-
ance

[17]mischievous

[18]spirit

[19]steal cream from

[20]interfere with the
operations of the
grinding mill

[21]in vain

[22]the froth on a cup
of ale

[23]female

[24]old woman's

[25]crabapple (used
to spice drinks)

[26]the fold of skin on
the neck

[27]company

[28]increase

[29]sneeze

Crowns him with flowers, and makes him all her joy.
And now they never meet in grove or green,
By fountain[13] clear, or spangled starlight sheen,[14]
30   But they do square,[15] that all their elves for fear
Creep into acorn cups and hide them there.
FAIRY: Either I mistake your shape and making[16] quite,
Or else you are that shrewd and knavish[17] sprite[18]
Call'd Robin Goodfellow.† Are not you he
35   That frights the maidens of the villagery,
Skim[19] milk, and sometimes labor in the quern,[20]
And bootless[21] make the breathless housewife churn,
And sometime make the drink to bear no barm,[22]
Mislead night-wanderers, laughing at their harm?
40   Those that Hobgoblin call you, and sweet Puck,
You do their work, and they shall have good luck.
Are not you he?
PUCK: Thou speakest aright:
I am that merry wanderer of the night.
45   I jest to Oberon, and make him smile,
When I a fat and bean-fed horse beguile,
Neighing in likeness of a filly[23] foal;
And sometime lurk I in a gossip's[24] bowl
In very likeness of a roasted crab,[25]
50   And, when she drinks, against her lips I bob,
And on her withered dewlap[26] pour the ale.
The wisest aunt, telling the saddest tale,
Sometime for three-foot stool mistaketh me;
Then slip I from her bum, down topples she,
55   And 'tailor'† cries, and falls into a cough;
And then the whole quire[27] hold their hips and laugh,
And waxen[28] in their mirth, and neeze,[29] and swear
A merrier hour was never wasted there.
But, room, fairy! here comes Oberon.
60 FAIRY: And here my mistress. Would that he were gone!

*Enter the King of Fairies, [Oberon] at one door, with his train,
and the Queen of Fairies, [Titania] at another, with hers.]*

OBERON: Ill met by moonlight, proud Titania.
TITANIA: What, jealous Oberon! Fairies, skip hence;

I have forsworn his bed and company.

OBERON: Tarry, rash wanton;[30] am not I thy lord?

65 TITANIA: Then I must be thy lady; but I know
When thou hast stolen away from fairy land,
And in the shape of Corin[†] sat all day,
Playing on pipes of corn, and versing love
To amorous Phillida.[†] Why art thou here,

70 Come from the farthest steep[31] of India?
But that, forsooth,[32] the bouncing[33] Amazon,[†]
Your buskin'd[34] mistress and your warrior love,
To Theseus must be wedded, and you come
To give their bed joy and prosperity?

75 OBERON: How canst thou thus, for shame, Titania,
Glance at my credit[35] with Hippolyta,
Knowing I know thy love to Theseus?
Didst not thou lead him through the glimmering night
From Perigouna,[†] whom he ravished?

80 And make him with fair Aegle[†] break his faith,
With Ariadne[†] and Antiopa?[†]

TITANIA: These are the forgeries[36] of jealousy;
And never, since the middle summer's spring,
Met we on hill, in dale, forest, or mead,[37]

85 By paved fountain, or by rushy[38] brook,
Or in the beached margent[39] of the sea,
To dance our ringlets[40] to the whistling wind,
But with thy brawls thou hast disturb'd our sport.
Therefore the winds, piping[41] to us in vain,

90 As in revenge, have suck'd up from the sea
Contagious fogs; which, falling in the land,
Hath every pelting[42] river made so proud
That they have overborne their continents.[43]
The ox hath therefore stretch'd his yoke in vain,

95 The ploughman lost his sweat, and the green corn[44]
Hath rotted ere his youth attain'd a beard;[45]
The fold[46] stands empty in the drowned field,
And crows are fatted with the murrion[47] flock;
The nine men's morris[48] is fill'd up with mud,

100 And the quaint mazes[49] in the wanton green,[50]
For lack of tread,[51] are undistinguishable.
The human mortals want[52] their winter here;

[30]*rebel*

[31]*limit, distance*

[32]*truly*

[33]*vigorous*

[34]*wearing hunting boots*

[35]*Question my good standing*

[36]*false stories*

[37]*meadow*

[38]*weed-covered; paved with weeds*

[39]*edge, border*

[40]*circular dances*

[41]*making music*

[42]*insignificant*

[43]*banks*

[44]*grain*

[45]*matured, grew old*

[46]*pen for livestock*

[47]*diseased*

[48]*playing area, field*

[49]*paths*

[50]*luxuriant grass*

[51]*walking; use*

[52]*lack*

No night is now with hymn or carol blest;
Therefore the moon, the governess of floods,
105   Pale in her anger, washes⁵³ all the air,
That rheumatic⁵⁴ diseases do abound.
And thorough this distemperature⁵⁵ we see
The seasons alter: hoary³⁶-headed frosts
Fall in the fresh lap of the crimson rose;
110   And on old Hiems'⁵⁷ thin and icy crown
An odorous⁵⁸ chaplet⁵⁹ of sweet summer buds
Is, as in mockery, set. The spring, the summer,
The childing⁶⁰ autumn, angry winter, change
Their wonted liveries;⁶¹ and the mazed⁶² world,
115   By their increase, now knows not which is which.
And this same progeny⁶³ of evils comes
From our debate, from our dissension;
We are their parents and original.
OBERON: Do you amend it, then; it lies in you.
120   Why should Titania cross her Oberon?
I do but beg a little changeling boy,
To be my henchman.⁶⁴
TITANIA: Set your heart at rest;
The fairy land buys not the child of me.
125   His mother was a votaress⁶⁵ of my order;
And, in the spiced Indian air, by night,
Full often hath she gossip'd by my side;
And sat with me on Neptune's† yellow sands,
Marking⁶⁶ the embarked traders⁶⁷ on the flood;⁶⁸
130   When we have laugh'd to see the sails conceive,
And grow big-bellied with the wanton wind;
Which she, with pretty and with swimming⁶⁹ gait⁷⁰
Following,⁷¹—her womb then rich with my young squire,—
Would imitate, and sail upon the land,
135   To fetch me trifles, and return again,
As from a voyage, rich with merchandise.
But she, being mortal, of that boy did die;
And for her sake do I rear up her boy;
And for her sake I will not part with him.
140   OBERON: How long within this wood intend you stay?
TITANIA: Perchance till after Theseus' wedding-day.
If you will patiently dance in our round,⁷²
And see our moonlight revels, go with us;

---

⁵³*dampens*

⁵⁴*flu-like*

⁵⁵*bad weather*

⁵⁶*white, aged*

⁵⁷*winter's*

⁵⁸*fragrant*

⁵⁹*wreath*

⁶⁰*fruitful*

⁶¹*customary outfits*

⁶²*confused, bewildered*

⁶³*offspring*

⁶⁴*an attendant, a messenger*

⁶⁵*devotee; priestess*

⁶⁶*Watching*

⁶⁷*merchant ships*

⁶⁸*ocean*

⁶⁹*graceful, flowing*

⁷⁰*walk*

⁷¹*Mimicking*

⁷²*circle dance*

If not, shun me, and I will spare your haunts.[73]

145 OBERON: Give me that boy, and I will go with thee.

TITANIA: Not for thy fairy kingdom. Fairies, away.

We shall chide[74] downright if I longer stay.

Exeunt [Titania with her train]

OBERON: Well, go thy way; thou shalt not from[75] this grove

Till I torment thee for this injury.

150 My gentle Puck, come hither. Thou rememberest

Since[76] once I sat upon a promontory,[77]

And heard a mermaid, on a dolphin's back

Uttering such dulcet[78] and harmonious breath,[79]

That the rude[80] sea grew civil[81] at her song,

155 And certain stars shot madly from their spheres[82]

To hear the sea-maid's music.

PUCK: I remember.

OBERON: That very time I saw, but thou couldst not,

Flying between the cold moon and the earth

160 Cupid all arm'd; a certain aim he took

At a fair vestal[83] throned by the west,

And loosed his love-shaft[84] smartly from his bow,

As[85] it should pierce a hundred thousand hearts;

But I might[86] see young Cupid's fiery shaft

165 Quench'd in the chaste beams of the watery moon;†

And the imperial votaress passed on,

In maiden meditation, fancy-free.

Yet mark'd I where the bolt of Cupid fell.

It fell upon a little western flower,

170 Before milk-white, now purple with love's wound,

And maidens call it love-in-idleness.[87]

Fetch me that flower, the herb I show'd thee once.

The juice of it on sleeping eye-lids laid

Will make or[88] man or woman madly dote

175 Upon the next live creature that it sees.

Fetch me this herb, and be thou here again

Ere the leviathan[89] can swim a league.

PUCK: I'll put a girdle round[90] about the earth

In forty minutes.   *[Exit Puck]*

180 OBERON: Having once this juice,

I'll watch Titania when she is asleep,

And drop the liquor of it in her eyes;

The next thing then she waking looks upon,

[73] *avoid*

[74] *fight*

[75] *go from*

[76] *When*

[77] *high ridge*

[78] *sweet sounding*

[79] *song*

[80] *rough*

[81] *peaceful*

[82] *orbits*

[83] *virgin*

[84] *golden arrow*

[85] *As though*

[86] *could*

[87] *pansy*

[88] *either*

[89] *sea creature*

[90] *circle around*

Be it on lion, bear, or wolf, or bull,

185   On meddling monkey, or on busy ape,

She shall pursue it with the soul of love.

And ere I take this charm from off her sight,

As I can take it with another herb,

I'll make her render up her page to me.

190   But who comes here? I am invisible;

And I will overhear their conference.

Enter Demetrius, Helena following him.

DEMETRIUS: I love thee not, therefore pursue me not.

Where is Lysander and fair Hermia?

The one I'll slay, the other slayeth me.

195   Thou told'st me they were stolen unto this wood,

And here am I, and wood[91] within this wood,

Because I cannot meet my Hermia.

Hence, get thee gone, and follow me no more.

HELENA: You draw me, you hard-hearted adamant;[92]

200   But yet you draw not iron, for my heart

Is true as steel. Leave you[93] your power to draw,[94]

And I shall have no power to follow you.

DEMETRIUS: Do I entice you? Do I speak you fair?

Or, rather, do I not in plainest truth

205   Tell you I do not nor I cannot love you?

HELENA: And even for that do I love you the more.

I am your spaniel; and, Demetrius,

The more you beat me, I will fawn on you.

Use me but as your spaniel, spurn me, strike me,

210   Neglect me, lose me; only give me leave,

Unworthy as I am, to follow you.

What worser place can I beg in your love,—

And yet a place of high respect with me,—

Than to be used as you use your dog?

215 DEMETRIUS: Tempt not too much the hatred of my spirit;

For I am sick when I do look on thee.

HELENA: And I am sick when I look not on you.

DEMETRIUS: You do impeach[95] your modesty too much

To leave the city and commit yourself

220   Into the hands of one that loves you not;

[91]*mad, insane*

[92]*stone with magnetic properties*

[93]*Abandon*

[94]*attract*

[95]*call into question*

To trust the opportunity of night,
And the ill counsel of a desert[96] place,
With the rich worth of your virginity.
HELENA: Your virtue is my privilege.[97] For that[98]
225   It is not night when I do see your face,
Therefore I think I am not in the night;
Nor doth this wood lack worlds of company,
For you, in my respect,[99] are all the world.
Then how can it be said I am alone
230   When all the world is here to look on me?
DEMETRIUS: I'll run from thee and hide me in the brakes,[100]
And leave thee to the mercy of wild beasts.
HELENA: The wildest hath not such a heart as you.
Run when you will; the story shall be changed:
235   Apollo flies, and Daphne holds the chase;†
The dove pursues the griffin;† the mild hind[101]
Makes speed to catch the tiger; bootless[102] speed,
When cowardice pursues and valour flies.
DEMETRIUS: I will not stay[103] thy questions; let me go;
240   Or, if thou follow me, do not believe
But I shall do thee mischief in the wood.
HELENA: Ay, in the temple, in the town, the field,
You do me mischief. Fie,[104] Demetrius!
Your wrongs do set a scandal on my sex.[105]
245   We cannot fight for love as men may do;
We should be woo'd, and were not made to woo.

                              [Exit Demetrius]

I'll follow thee, and make a heaven of hell,
To die upon the hand I love so well.

                              Exit [Helena]

OBERON: Fare thee well, nymph; ere he do leave this grove,
250   Thou shalt fly[106] him, and he shall seek thy love.

[Re-]enter Puck
Hast thou the flower there? Welcome, wanderer.
PUCK: Ay, there it is.
OBERON: I pray thee give it me.
I know a bank where the wild thyme blows,
255   Where oxlips[107] and the nodding violet grows,
Quite over-canopied with luscious woodbine,[108]

[96]*deserted*

[97]*protection*

[98]*Because*

[99]*perspective*

[100]*thickets*

[101]*doe*

[102]*useless*

[103]*endure*

[104]*Shame*

[105]*disgrace females*

[106]*flee*

[107]*flowers (similar to primrose)*

[108]*honeysuckle*

[109]large white
 roses

[110]roses

[111]Lounged

[112]Garment, cloak

[113]spies

[114]Do

     With sweet musk-roses,[109] and with eglantine;[110]
     There sleeps Titania sometime of the night,
     Lull'd[111] in these flowers with dances and delight;
260 And there the snake throws her enamell'd skin,
     Weed[112] wide enough to wrap a fairy in;
     And with the juice of this I'll streak her eyes,
     And make her full of hateful fantasies.
     Take thou some of it, and seek through this grove:
265 A sweet Athenian lady is in love
     With a disdainful youth; anoint his eyes;
     But do it when the next thing he espies[113]
     May be the lady. Thou shalt know the man
     By the Athenian garments he hath on.
270 Effect[114] it with some care, that he may prove
     More fond on her than she upon her love.
     And look thou meet me ere the first cock crow.
   Puck: Fear not, my lord; your servant shall do so.

                 Exeunt

SCENE II
[Another part of the wood]

Enter Titania, Queen of Fairies, with her train

[1]circle dance

[2]worms

[3]bats

   Titania: Come now, a roundel[1] and a fairy song;
     Then, for the third part of a minute, hence:
     Some to kill cankers[2] in the musk-rose buds;
     Some war with rere-mice[3] for their leathern wings,
5   To make my small elves coats; and some keep back
     The clamorous owl that nightly hoots and wonders
     At our quaint spirits. Sing me now asleep;
     Then to your offices, and let me rest. *Let me*
                   sleep & do
                   your work

   The Fairies Sing

   First Fairy: *[song]*
10 You spotted snakes with double tongue,

Thorny hedgehogs, be not seen;
Newts and blind-worms,† do no wrong,
Come not near our fairy Queen.

CHORUS
Philomel† with melody
15   Sing in our sweet lullaby.
Lulla, lulla, lullaby; lulla, lulla, lullaby.
Never harm
Nor spell nor charm
Come our lovely lady nigh.
20   So good night, with lullaby.

SECOND FAIRY: Weaving spiders, come not here;
Hence, you long-legg'd spinners, hence.
Beetles black, approach not near;
Worm nor snail do no offence.

CHORUS
25   Philomel with melody, &c.

FIRST FAIRY: Hence away; now all is well.
One aloof⁴ stand sentinel.⁵   ⁴*distant*
                    [Exeunt Fairies, Titania] Sleeps   ⁵*guard*

Enter Oberon [and squeezes the flower on Titania's eyelids]

OBERON: What thou seest when thou dost wake,
Do it for thy true-love take;
30   Love and languish for his sake.
Be it ounce,⁶ or cat, or bear,   ⁶*wildcat*
Pard,⁷ or boar with bristled hair,   ⁷*Leopard*
In thy eye that shall appear
When thou wakest, it is thy dear.
35   Wake when some vile thing is near.   *[Exit]*

Enter Lysander and Hermia

LYSANDER: Fair love, you faint with wandering in the wood;

⁸*truth*

⁹*wait*

And, to speak troth,⁸ I have forgot our way;
We'll rest us, Hermia, if you think it good,
And tarry⁹ for the comfort of the day.

40 HERMIA: Be it so, Lysander: find you out a bed,
For I upon this bank will rest my head.

LYSANDER: One turf shall serve as pillow for us both;
One heart, one bed, two bosoms, and one troth.

HERMIA: Nay, good Lysander; for my sake, my dear,

45   Lie further off yet; do not lie so near.

LYSANDER: O, take the sense, sweet, of my innocence!†
Love takes the meaning in love's conference.¹⁰

¹⁰*"Love speaks for
    itself between
    two lovers."*

I mean, that my heart unto yours is knit,
So that but one heart we can make of it;

50   Two bosoms interchained with an oath,
So then two bosoms and a single troth.
Then by your side no bed-room me deny,
For lying so, Hermia, I do not lie.

HERMIA: Lysander riddles very prettily.

¹¹*curse*

55   Now much beshrew¹¹ my manners and my pride,
If Hermia meant to say Lysander lied!
But, gentle friend, for love and courtesy
Lie further off, in human¹² modesty;

¹²*humane,
    courteous*

Such separation as may well be said

60   Becomes a virtuous bachelor and a maid,
So far be distant; and good night, sweet friend.
Thy love ne'er alter till thy sweet life end!

LYSANDER: Amen, amen, to that fair prayer say I;
And then end life when I end loyalty!

65   Here is my bed; sleep give thee all his rest!

HERMIA: With half that wish the wisher's eyes be press'd!

They sleep

Enter Puck

PUCK: Through the forest have I gone,
But Athenian found I none,
On whose eyes I might approve
This flower's force in stirring love.

70   Night and silence.—Who is here?
Weeds of Athens he doth wear:

This is he, my master said,
Despised the Athenian maid;
And here the maiden, sleeping sound,
75 On the dank and dirty ground.
Pretty soul! she durst not lie
Near this lack-love, this kill-courtesy.
Churl,[13] upon thy eyes I throw
All the power this charm doth owe:[14]
80 When thou wakest let love forbid
Sleep his seat on thy eyelid.
So awake when I am gone;
For I must now to Oberon.   *Exit*

Enter Demetrius and Helena, running

HELENA: Stay, though thou kill me, sweet Demetrius.
85 DEMETRIUS: I charge thee, hence, and do not haunt me thus.
HELENA: O, wilt thou darkling[15] leave me? Do not so.
DEMETRIUS: Stay on thy peril;[16] I alone will go.
                                            Exit Demetrius
HELENA: O, I am out of breath in this fond chase!
The more my prayer, the lesser is my grace.
90 Happy is Hermia, wheresoe'er she lies,
For she hath blessed and attractive eyes.
How came her eyes so bright? Not with salt tears;
If so, my eyes are oft'ner wash'd than hers.
No, no, I am as ugly as a bear,
95 For beasts that meet me run away for fear;
Therefore no marvel though Demetrius
Do, as a monster, fly my presence thus.
What wicked and dissembling glass[17] of mine
Made me compare[18] with Hermia's sphery eyne?[19]
100 But who is here? Lysander! on the ground!
Dead, or asleep? I see no blood, no wound.
Lysander, if you live, good sir, awake.
LYSANDER: [*Waking*] And run through fire I will for thy sweet
        sake.
105 Transparent Helena! Nature shows art,[20]
That through thy bosom makes me see thy heart.
Where is Demetrius? O, how fit a word

[13]*Villain*

[14]*own*

[15]*in the dark*

[16]*"Stay here or you will risk danger if you follow me."*

[17]*mirror*

[18]*compete*

[19]*eyes*

[20]*magical skill*

Is that vile name to perish on my sword!

HELENA: Do not say so, Lysander; say not so.

110 What though he love your Hermia? Lord, what though?
Yet Hermia still loves you; then be content.

LYSANDER: Content with Hermia! No: I do repent
The tedious minutes I with her have spent.

115 Not Hermia but Helena I love:
Who will not change a raven for a dove?
The will of man is by his reason sway'd,
And reason says you are the worthier maid.
Things growing are not ripe until their season;

120 So I, being young, till now ripe not to reason;
And touching now the point of human skill,

²¹*guide*

Reason becomes the marshal²¹ to my will,
And leads me to your eyes, where I o'erlook
Love's stories, written in Love's richest book.

²²*sharp*

125 HELENA: Wherefore was I to this keen²² mockery born?
When at your hands did I deserve this scorn?
Is't not enough, is't not enough, young man,
That I did never, no, nor never can,
Deserve a sweet look from Demetrius' eye,

130 But you must flout my insufficiency?

²³*indeed*

Good troth, you do me wrong, good sooth,²³ you do,
In such disdainful manner me to woo.

²⁴*necessarily*

But fare you well; perforce²⁴ I must confess

²⁵*courtesy*

I thought you lord of more true gentleness.²⁵

135 O, that a lady of one man refused
Should of another therefore be abused!   *Exit*

LYSANDER: She sees not Hermia. Hermia, sleep thou there;
And never mayst thou come Lysander near!

²⁶*overabundance*

For, as a surfeit²⁶ of the sweetest things

140 The deepest loathing to the stomach brings,
Or as the heresies that men do leave
Are hated most of those they did deceive,†
So thou, my surfeit and my heresy,
Of all be hated, but the most of me!

145 And, all my powers, address your love and might
To honor Helen, and to be her knight!   *Exit*

HERMIA: [*Awaking*] Help me, Lysander, help me; do thy best
To pluck this crawling serpent from my breast.

Ay me, for pity! What a dream was here!
150 Lysander, look how I do quake with fear.
Methought a serpent eat my heart away,
And you sat smiling at his cruel prey.[27]
Lysander! What, removed? Lysander! lord!
What, out of hearing? gone? No sound, no word?
155 Alack, where are you? Speak, an if you hear;
Speak, of[28] all loves! I swoon almost with fear.
No? Then I well perceive you are not nigh.
Either death or you I'll find immediately.

Exit

[27] *attack*

[28] *For the sake of*

ACT III

SCENE I
[The wood]

Enter the clowns, [Quince, Snug, Bottom, Flute, Snout, and Starveling]

BOTTOM: Are we all met?

QUINCE: Pat,[1] pat; and here's a marvellous convenient place
for our rehearsal. This green plot shall be our stage, this
hawthorn-brake[2] our tiring-house;[3] and we will do it in
5   action, as we will do it before the Duke.

BOTTOM: Peter Quince,—

QUINCE: What sayest thou, bully[4] Bottom?

BOTTOM: There are things in this comedy of Pyramus and
Thisbe that will never please. First, Pyramus must draw a
10   sword to kill himself; which the ladies cannot abide. How
answer you that?

SNOUT: By'r lakin,[5] a parlous[6] fear.

STARVELING: I believe we must leave the killing out, when all
is done.

15 BOTTOM: Not a whit;[7] I have a device to make all well. Write
me a prologue; and let the prologue seem to say we will
do no harm with our swords, and that Pyramus is not
kill'd indeed; and for the more better assurance, tell them
that I Pyramus am not Pyramus, but Bottom the weaver.
20   This will put them out of fear.

QUINCE: Well, we will have such a prologue; and it shall be
written in eight and six.†

BOTTOM: No, make it two more; let it be written in eight and
eight.

25 SNOUT: Will not the ladies be afeard of the lion?

STARVELING: I fear it, I promise you.

---

[1] *Right on time*

[2] *thicket*

[3] *dressing room*

[4] *good fellow*

[5] *"By our Lady"*
(an oath)

[6] *perilous*

[7] *Not at all*

BOTTOM: Masters, you ought to consider with yourselves to bring in—God shield us!—a lion among ladies is a most dreadful thing; for there is not a more fearful wild-fowl

30   than your lion living; and we ought to look to't.

SNOUT: Therefore another prologue must tell he is not a lion.

BOTTOM: Nay, you must name his name, and half his face must be seen through the lion's neck; and he himself

35   must speak through, saying thus, or to the same defect:[8] —'Ladies,' —or 'Fair ladies,—I would wish you'—or 'I would request you' —or 'I would entreat you,—not to fear, not to tremble. My life for yours! If you think I come hither as a lion, it were pity of[9] my life. No, I am

40   no such thing; I am a man as other men are.' And there, indeed, let him name his name, and tell them plainly he is Snug the joiner.

QUINCE: Well, it shall be so. But there is two hard things; that is, to bring the moonlight into a chamber; for, you

45   know, Pyramus and Thisbe meet by moonlight.

SNOUT: Doth the moon shine that night we play our play?

BOTTOM: A calendar, a calendar! Look in the almanack; find out moonshine, find out moonshine.

QUINCE: Yes, it doth shine that night.

50 BOTTOM: Why, then may you leave a casement[10] of the great chamber window, where we play, open; and the moon may shine in at the casement.

QUINCE: Ay; or else one must come in with a bush of thorns† and a lantern, and say he comes to disfigure,[11]

55   or to present,[12] the person of moonshine. Then, there is another thing: we must have a wall in the great chamber; for Pyramus and Thisbe, says the story, did talk through the chink of a wall.

SNOUT: You can never bring in a wall. What say you,

60   Bottom?

BOTTOM: Some man or other must present Wall; and let him have some plaster, or some loam, or some rough-cast about him, to signify wall; and let him hold his fingers thus, and through that cranny shall Pyramus and

65   Thisbe whisper.

[8] "effect"

[9] threat to

[10] pane

[11] "figure"

[12] represent

QUINCE: If that may be, then all is well. Come, sit down, every mother's son, and rehearse your parts. Pyramus, you begin; when you have spoken your speech, enter into that brake; and so every one according to his cue.

Enter Robin [Goodfellow (Puck)]

70 PUCK: What hempen home-spuns[13] have we swagg'ring here,
So near the cradle[14] of the fairy queen?
What, a play toward![15] I'll be an auditor;
An actor too perhaps, if I see cause.
QUINCE: Speak, Pyramus. Thisbe, stand forth.
75 BOTTOM: Thisbe, the flowers of odious[16] savors sweet—
QUINCE: 'Odours,' odours!
BOTTOM: —odours savors sweet;
So hath thy breath, my dearest Thisbe dear.
But hark, a voice! Stay thou but here awhile,
80 And by and by[17] I will to thee appear.

                              Exit Pyramus [Bottom]

PUCK: A stranger Pyramus than e'er play'd here!

                                        [Exit]

FLUTE: Must I speak now?
QUINCE: Ay, marry, must you; for you must understand he goes but to see a noise that he heard, and is to come
85 again.
FLUTE: Most radiant Pyramus, most lily-white of hue,
Of color like the red rose on triumphant brier,
Most brisky[18] juvenal,[19] and eke[20] most lovely Jew,†
As true as truest horse, that would never tire,
90 I'll meet thee, Pyramus, at Ninny's tomb.
QUINCE: 'Ninus'† tomb,' man! Why, you must not speak that yet; that you answer to Pyramus. You speak all your part at once, cues, and all. Pyramus enter: your cue is past; it is 'never tire.'
95 FLUTE: O—As true as truest horse, that yet would never tire.

[Re-enter Puck, and Bottom with an ass's head]

[13]*country bumpkins (wearing coarse, hemp clothing)*

[14]*sleeping place*

[15]*in the making*

[16]*"odorous"*

[17]*soon*

[18]*lively*

[19]*youth*

[20]*also*

BOTTOM: If I were fair, Thisbe, I were[21] only thine.
QUINCE: O monstrous! O strange! We are haunted. Pray, masters! fly, masters! Help!

                    The clowns all exit. [Puck remains.]

22in circles

PUCK: I'll follow you; I'll lead you about a round,[22]
100   Through bog, through bush, through brake, through brier;
       Sometime a horse I'll be, sometime a hound,
       A hog, a headless bear, sometime a fire;†
       And neigh, and bark, and grunt, and roar, and burn,
       Like horse, hound, hog, bear, fire, at every turn.

                                                    Exit

Enter [Bottom] with the Asshead

105   BOTTOM: Why do they run away? This is a knavery of them
       to make me afeard.

[Re-]enter Snout

SNOUT: O Bottom, thou art changed! What do I see on thee?
BOTTOM: What do you see? You see an ass-head of your
110   own,† do you?   *[Exit Snout]*

[Re-]enter Peter Quince

23transformed

QUINCE: Bless thee, Bottom, bless thee! Thou art translated.[23]
                                                    [Exit]

BOTTOM: I see their knavery: this is to make an ass of me;
       to fright me, if they could. But I will not stir from this
       place, do what they can; I will walk up and down here,
115   and will sing, that they shall hear I am not afraid.
                                                    [Sings]

24male blackbird

25song bird

26musical pipe

           The ousel cock,[24] so black of hue,
                With orange-tawny bill,
           The throstle[25] with his note so true,
                The wren with little quill.[26]

120   TITANIA: *[Awakening]* What angel wakes me from my
       flowery bed?
       BOTTOM: *[Sings]*

The finch, the sparrow, and the lark,
    The plain-song[27] cuckoo gray,
Whose note full many a man doth mark,
125   And dares not answer nay;[28†]—

for, indeed, who would set his wit to[29] so foolish a bird?
Who would give a bird the lie,[30] though he cry 'cuckoo'
never so?[31]

TITANIA: I pray thee, gentle mortal, sing again.
130   Mine ear is much enamored of thy note;
So is mine eye enthralled to thy shape;
And thy fair virtue's force perforce doth move me,
On the first view to say, to swear, I love thee.

BOTTOM: Methinks, mistress, you should have little reason for
135   that. And yet, to say the truth, reason and love keep little
company together now-a-days. The more the pity that
some honest neighbors will not make them friends. Nay, I
can gleek[32] upon occasion.

TITANIA: Thou art as wise as thou art beautiful.

140 BOTTOM: Not so, neither; but if I had wit enough to get out of
this wood, I have enough to serve mine own turn.[33]

TITANIA: Out of this wood do not desire to go;
Thou shalt remain here whether thou wilt or no.
I am a spirit of no common rate;[34]
145   The summer still[35] doth tend upon my state;[36]
And I do love thee; therefore, go with me.
I'll give thee fairies to attend on thee;
And they shall fetch thee jewels from the deep,
And sing, while thou on pressed flowers dost sleep;
150   And I will purge thy mortal grossness[37] so
That thou shalt like an airy spirit go.
Peaseblossom! Cobweb! Moth! and Mustardseed!

Enter four Fairies: Peaseblossom, Cobweb, Moth, and Mustardseed

PEASEBLOSSOM: Ready.
COBWEB: And I.
155 MOTH: And I.
MUSTARDSEED: And I.
ALL: Where shall we go?

---

[27] *simply singing*

[28] *deny*

[29] *pay attention to*

[30] *accuse the bird of lying*

[31] *constantly*

[32] *make jokes*

[33] *purpose*

[34] *rank*

[35] *always*

[36] *serve me*

[37] *earthly heaviness; earthly being*

TITANIA: Be kind and courteous to this gentleman;
           Hop in his walks, and gambol[38] in his eyes;
160   Feed him with apricocks[39] and dewberries,[40]
           With purple grapes, green figs, and mulberries;
           The honey-bags steal from the humble-bees,[41]
           And for night-tapers[42] crop their waxen thighs,
           And light them at the fiery glow-worm's eyes,
165   To have[43] my love to bed and to arise;
           And pluck the wings from painted butterflies,
           To fan the moonbeams from his sleeping eyes.
           Nod to him, elves, and do him courtesies.
PEASEBLOSSOM: Hail, mortal!
170 COBWEB: Hail!
MOTH: Hail!
MUSTARDSEED: Hail!
BOTTOM: I cry your worships mercy, heartily; I beseech
         your worship's name.
175 COBWEB: Cobweb.
BOTTOM: I shall desire you of more acquaintance, good
         Master Cobweb. If I cut my finger,† I shall make bold
         with you. Your name, honest gentleman?
PEASEBLOSSOM: Peaseblossom.
180 BOTTOM: I pray you, commend me to Mistress Squash,
         your mother, and to Master Peascod, your father.
         Good Master Peaseblossom, I shall desire you of more
         acquaintance too. Your name, I beseech you, sir?
MUSTARDSEED: Mustardseed.
185 BOTTOM: Good Master Mustardseed, I know your patience[44]
         well. That same cowardly giant-like ox-beef hath
         devoured many a gentleman of your house. I prom-
         ise you your kindred hath made my eyes water ere
         now. I desire your more acquaintance, good Master
190   Mustardseed.
TITANIA: Come, wait upon him; lead him to my bower.
         The moon, methinks, looks with a watery eye;
         And when she weeps, weeps every little flower;†
         Lamenting some enforced[45] chastity.
195   Tie up my love's tongue, bring him silently.

                                                      [Exeunt]

[38]frolic

[39]apricots

[40]blackberries

[41]bumblebees

[42]candles

[43]lead

[44]suffering

[45]violated; forced

SCENE II
[Another part of the wood]

Enter The King of Fairies [Oberon]

OBERON:　I wonder if Titania be awaked;
　　　Then, what it was that next came in her eye,
　　　Which she must dote on in extremity.

Enter Puck

　　　Here comes my messenger.
5　　　　　How now, mad spirit!
　　　What night-rule[1] now about this haunted grove?
PUCK:　My mistress with a monster is in love.
　　　Near to her close[2] and consecrated[3] bower,
　　　While she was in her dull[4] and sleeping hour,
10　　A crew of patches,[5] rude mechanicals,[6]
　　　That work for bread upon Athenian stalls,[7]
　　　Were met together to rehearse a play,
　　　Intended for great Theseus' nuptial-day.
　　　The shallowest thick-skin of that barren sort,
15　　Who Pyramus presented, in their sport
　　　Forsook his scene[8] and ent'red in a brake;
　　　When I did him at this advantage take,
　　　An ass's nole[9] I fixed on his head.
　　　Anon his Thisbe must be answered,
20　　And forth my mimic[10] comes. When they him spy,
　　　As wild geese that the creeping fowler[11] eye,
　　　Or russet-pated choughs,[12] many in sort,
　　　Rising and cawing at the gun's report,
　　　Sever[13] themselves and madly sweep the sky,
25　　So, at his sight, away his fellows fly;
　　　And at our stamp here, o'er and o'er one falls;
　　　He murder cries, and help from Athens calls.
　　　Their sense thus weak, lost with their fears thus strong,
　　　Made senseless things begin to do them wrong,
30　　For briers and thorns at their apparel snatch;
　　　Some sleeves, some hats, from yielders[14] all things catch.
　　　I led them on in this distracted fear,
　　　And left sweet Pyramus translated there;

[1]*commotion*

[2]*private*

[3]*blessed*

[4]*drowsy*

[5]*fools*

[6]*workers*

[7]*market booths*

[8]*stage*

[9]*head*

[10]*comedic actor*

[11]*bird hunter*

[12]*jackdaws (gray birds similar to crows)*

[13]*scatter*

[14]*timid people*

When in that moment, so it came to pass,

35   Titania waked, and straightway loved an ass.

OBERON: This falls out[15] better than I could devise.

But hast thou yet latch'd[16] the Athenian's eyes

With the love-juice, as I did bid thee do?

PUCK: I took him sleeping,—that is finish'd too,—

40   And the Athenian woman by his side;

That, when he waked, of force[17] she must be eyed.

Enter Demetrius and Hermia

OBERON: Stand close;[18] this is the same Athenian.

PUCK: This is the woman, but not this the man.

DEMETRIUS: O, why rebuke you him that loves you so?

45   Lay breath so bitter on your bitter foe.

HERMIA: Now I but chide, but I should use thee worse,

For thou, I fear, hast given me cause to curse.

If thou hast slain Lysander in his sleep,

Being o'er shoes in blood, plunge in the deep,

50   And kill me too.

The sun was not so true unto the day

As he to me. Would he have stolen away

From sleeping Hermia? I'll believe as soon

This whole[19] earth may be bored, and that the moon

55   May through the centre creep and so displease

Her brother's† noontide[20] with the Antipodes.†

It cannot be but thou hast murder'd him;

So should a murderer look, so dead, so grim.

DEMETRIUS: So should the murdered look; and so should I,

60   Pierced through the heart with your stern cruelty;

Yet you, the murderer, look as bright, as clear,

As yonder Venus in her glimmering sphere.

HERMIA: What's this to my Lysander? Where is he?

Ah, good Demetrius, wilt thou give him me?

65 DEMETRIUS: I had rather give his carcass to my hounds.

HERMIA: Out, dog! out, cur! Thou drivest me past the bounds

Of maiden's patience. Hast thou slain him, then?

Henceforth be never number'd among men!

O, once tell true; tell true, even for my sake!

70   Durst thou have look'd upon him being awake,

---

[15]*happens*

[16]*moistened*

[17]*necessity*

[18]*hidden*

[19]*solid*

[20]*midday*

And hast thou kill'd him sleeping? O brave touch!
Could not a worm,[21] an adder,[22] do so much?
An adder did it; for with doubler[23] tongue
Than thine, thou serpent, never adder stung.

75 DEMETRIUS: You spend your passion on a misprised[24] mood:
I am not guilty of Lysander's blood;
Nor is he dead, for aught that I can tell.

HERMIA: I pray thee, tell me then that he is well.

DEMETRIUS: An if I could, what should I get therefore?

80 HERMIA: A privilege, never to see me more.
And from thy hated presence part I so;
See me no more, whether he be dead or no.

                                                    Exit

DEMETRIUS: There is no following her in this fierce vein;
Here, therefore, for a while I will remain.
85 So sorrow's heaviness[25] doth heavier grow
For debt that bankrupt sleep doth sorrow owe;
Which now in some slight measure it will pay,
If for his tender here I make some stay.

                        Lie[s] down [and sleeps]

OBERON: What hast thou done? Thou hast mistaken quite,
90 And laid the love-juice on some true-love's sight.
Of thy misprision[26] must perforce ensue
Some true love turn'd, and not a false turn'd true.

PUCK: Then fate o'er-rules, that, one man holding troth,
A million fail, confounding oath on oath.

95 OBERON: About the wood go swifter than the wind,
And Helena of Athens look[27] thou find;
All fancy-sick[28] she is and pale of cheer,[29]
With sighs of love that costs the fresh blood dear.
By some illusion see thou bring her here;
100 I'll charm his eyes against she do appear.

PUCK: I go, I go; look how I go,
Swifter than arrow from the Tartar's[†] bow.

                                                    Exit

OBERON: Flower of this purple dye,
Hit with Cupid's archery,
105 Sink in apple[30] of his eye.
When his love he doth espy,
Let her shine as gloriously

[21]*serpent*

[22]*venomous snake*

[23]*more forked*

[24]*misplaced*

[25]*sadness*

[26]*mistake*

[27]*be sure*

[28]*lovesick*

[29]*complexion*

[30]*pupil*

As the Venus of the sky.
When thou wakest, if she be by,
110   Beg of her for remedy.

[Re-]enter Puck

PUCK: Captain of our fairy band,
     Helena is here at hand,
     And the youth, mistook by me
     Pleading for a lover's fee;[31]
115   Shall we their fond[32] pageant see?
     Lord, what fools these mortals be!
OBERON: Stand aside. The noise they make
     Will cause Demetrius to awake.
PUCK: Then will two at once woo one.
120   That must needs be sport alone;
     And those things do best please me
     That befall[33] preposterously.

Enter Lysander and Helena

LYSANDER: Why should you think that I should woo in scorn?
     Scorn and derision[34] never come in tears.
125   Look when I vow, I weep; and vows so born,
     In their nativity all truth appears.
     How can these things in me seem scorn to you,
     Bearing the badge of faith,† to prove them true?
HELENA: You do advance[35] your cunning more and more.
130   When truth kills truth, O devilish-holy fray!
     These vows are Hermia's. Will you give her o'er?
     Weigh oath with oath, and you will nothing weigh:
     Your vows to her and me, put in two scales,
     Will even weigh; and both as light as tales.
135 LYSANDER: I had no judgment when to her I swore.
HELENA: Nor none, in my mind, now you give her o'er.
LYSANDER: Demetrius loves her, and he loves not you.
DEMETRIUS: (*Awaking*) O Helen, goddess, nymph, perfect,
     divine!
140   To what, my love, shall I compare thine eyne?
     Crystal is muddy. O, how ripe in show

[31]*reward*

[32]*foolish*

[33]*occur*

[34]*ridicule*

[35]*increase*

Thy lips, those kissing cherries, tempting grow!
That pure congealed white, high Taurus'† snow,
Fann'd with the eastern wind, turns to a crow[36]
145 When thou hold'st up thy hand. O, let me kiss
This princess of pure white, this seal[37] of bliss!
Helena: O spite! O hell! I see you all are bent
To set against me for your merriment.
If you were civil and knew courtesy,
150 You would not do me thus much injury.
Can you not hate me, as I know you do,
But you must join in souls to mock me too?
If you were men, as men you are in show,
You would not use a gentle lady so:
155 To vow, and swear, and superpraise[38] my parts,
When I am sure you hate me with your hearts.
You both are rivals, and love Hermia;
And now both rivals, to mock Helena.
A trim[39] exploit, a manly enterprise,
160 To conjure tears up in a poor maid's eyes
With your derision! None of noble sort
Would so offend a virgin, and extort[40]
A poor soul's patience, all to make you sport.
Lysander: You are unkind, Demetrius; be not so;
165 For you love Hermia. This you know I know;
And here, with all good will, with all my heart,
In Hermia's love I yield you up my part;
And yours of Helena to me bequeath,[41]
Whom I do love and will do till my death.
170 Helena: Never did mockers waste more idle breath.
Demetrius: Lysander, keep thy Hermia; I will none.[42]
If e'er I loved her, all that love is gone.
My heart to her but as guest-wise[43] sojourn'd,[44]
And now to Helen is it home return'd,
175 There to remain.
Lysander: Helen, it is not so.
Demetrius: Disparage not the faith thou dost not know,
Lest, to thy peril, thou aby it dear.[45]
Look where thy love comes; yonder is thy dear.

Enter Hermia

[36]*black in color*

[37]*pledge*

[38]*excessively praise*

[39]*fine*

[40]*torture*

[41]*give up*

[42]*having nothing to do with her*

[43]*a guest*

[44]*visited*

[45]*pay dearly*

180 HERMIA: Dark night, that from the eye his function takes,
    The ear more quick of apprehension makes;
    Wherein it doth impair the seeing sense,
    It pays the hearing double recompense.[46]
    Thou art not by mine eye, Lysander, found;
185   Mine ear, I thank it, brought me to thy sound.
    But why unkindly didst thou leave me so?
LYSANDER: Why should he stay whom love doth press to go?
HERMIA: What love could press Lysander from my side?
LYSANDER: Lysander's love, that would not let him bide,[47]
190   Fair Helena, who more engilds[48] the night
    Than all yon fiery oes and eyes of light.[49]
    Why seek'st thou me? Could not this make thee know,
    The hate I bare thee made me leave thee so?
HERMIA: You speak not as you think; it cannot be.
195 HELENA: Lo, she is one of this confederacy!
    Now I perceive they have conjoin'd all three
    To fashion this false sport, in spite of me.
    Injurious Hermia! most ungrateful maid!
    Have you conspired, have you with these contrived,
200   To bait[50] me with this foul derision?
    Is all the counsel that we two have shared,
    The sisters' vows, the hours that we have spent,
    When we have chid[51] the hasty-footed time
    For parting us,—O, is all forgot?
205   All school-days' friendship, childhood innocence?
    We, Hermia, like two artificial gods,
    Have with our needles created both one flower,
    Both on one sampler,[52] sitting on one cushion,
    Both warbling of one song, both in one key;
210   As if our hands, our sides, voices, and minds,
    Had been incorporate.[53] So we grew together,
    Like to a double cherry, seeming parted,
    But yet an union in partition,
    Two lovely berries moulded on one stem;
215   So, with two seeming bodies, but one heart;
    Two of the first, like coats[54] in heraldry,
    Due but to one, and crowned with one crest.
    And will you rent our ancient love asunder,
    To join with men in scorning your poor friend?

[46]compensation

[47]wait

[48]brightens

[49]stars

[50]torment

[51]scolded

[52]piece of embroidery

[53]as one

[54]coats of arms

220   It is not friendly, 'tis not maidenly;
        Our sex, as well as I, may chide you for it,
        Though I alone do feel the injury.
     HERMIA: I am amazed at your passionate words;
        I scorn you not; it seems that you scorn me.
225 HELENA: Have you not set Lysander, as in scorn,
        To follow me and praise my eyes and face?
        And made your other love, Demetrius,
        Who even but now did spurn me with his foot,
        To call me goddess, nymph, divine, and rare,
230   Precious, celestial? Wherefore speaks he this
        To her he hates? And wherefore doth Lysander
        Deny your love, so rich within his soul,
        And tender[55] me, forsooth, affection,   [55]offer
        But by your setting on, by your consent?
235   What though I be not so in grace[56] as you,   [56]favor
        So hung upon with love, so fortunate,
        But miserable most, to love unloved?
        This you should pity rather than despise.
     HERMIA: I understand not what you mean by this.
240 HELENA: Ay, do, persever,[57] counterfeit sad[58] looks,   [57]persevere, over-
        Make mouths[59] upon me when I turn my back,   come
        Wink each at other; hold the sweet jest up;   [58]serious
        This sport, well carried, shall be chronicled.
        If you have any pity, grace, or manners,   [59]faces
245   You would not make me such an argument.[60]   [60]laughingstock
        But fare ye well; 'tis partly my own fault,
        Which death, or absence, soon shall remedy.
     LYSANDER: Stay, gentle Helena; hear my excuse;
        My love, my life, my soul, fair Helena!
250 HELENA: O excellent!
     HERMIA: Sweet, do not scorn her so.
     DEMETRIUS: If she cannot entreat, I can compel.[61]   [61]force (you to
     LYSANDER: Thou canst compel no more than she entreat;   stop)
        Thy threats have no more strength than her weak prayers
255   Helen, I love thee, by my life, I do;
        I swear by that which I will lose for thee
        To prove him false that says I love thee not.
     DEMETRIUS: I say I love thee more than he can do.

62"step outside"
  (a challenge)

63Ethiopian

64pretend

65Let go

66truly

67before

68trickster

69worm that eats
  flower buds

70imitation

LYSANDER: If thou say so, withdraw,62 and prove it too.

260 DEMETRIUS: Quick, come.

HERMIA: Lysander, whereto tends all this?

LYSANDER: Away, you Ethiope!63†

DEMETRIUS: No, no, he will

    Seem to break loose—take on64 as you would follow,

265   But yet come not. You are a tame man; go!

LYSANDER: Hang off,65 thou cat, thou burr; vile thing, let loose,

    Or I will shake thee from me like a serpent.

HERMIA: Why are you grown so rude? What change is this,

    Sweet love?

270 LYSANDER: Thy love! Out, tawny Tartar, out!

    Out, loathed medicine! O hated potion, hence!

HERMIA: Do you not jest?

HELENA: Yes, sooth;66 and so do you.

LYSANDER: Demetrius, I will keep my word with thee.

275 DEMETRIUS: I would I had your bond; for I perceive

    A weak bond holds you; I'll not trust your word.

LYSANDER: What, should I hurt her, strike her, kill her dead?

    Although I hate her, I'll not harm her so.

HERMIA: What! Can you do me greater harm than hate?

280   Hate me! wherefore? O me! what news, my love?

    Am not I Hermia? Are not you Lysander?

    I am as fair now as I was erewhile.67

    Since night you loved me; yet since night you left me.

    Why then, you left me,—O, the gods forbid!—

285   In earnest, shall I say?

LYSANDER: Ay, by my life!

    And never did desire to see thee more.

    Therefore be out of hope, of question, of doubt;

    Be certain, nothing truer; 'tis no jest

290   That I do hate thee and love Helena.

HERMIA: O me! you juggler!68 you cankerblossom!69

    You thief of love! What! Have you come by night,

    And stolen my love's heart from him?

HELENA: Fine, i' faith!

295   Have you no modesty, no maiden shame,

    No touch of bashfulness? What! Will you tear

    Impatient answers from my gentle tongue?

    Fie, fie! you counterfeit, you puppet70† you!

HERMIA: 'Puppet!' why so? Ay, that way goes the game.
300   Now I perceive that she hath made compare
        Between our statures; she hath urged her height;
        And with her personage, her tall personage,
        Her height, forsooth, she hath prevail'd with him.
        And are you grown so high in his esteem
305   Because I am so dwarfish and so low?
        How low am I, thou painted[71] maypole?[72] Speak.
        How low am I? I am not yet so low
        But that my nails can reach unto thine eyes.
HELENA: I pray you, though you mock me, gentlemen,
310   Let her not hurt me. I was never curst;[73]
        I have no gift at all in shrewishness;[74]
        I am a right[75] maid for my cowardice;
        Let her not strike me. You perhaps may think,
        Because she is something[76] lower than myself,
315   That I can match her.
HERMIA: 'Lower' hark, again.
HELENA: Good Hermia, do not be so bitter with me.
        I evermore did love you, Hermia,
        Did ever keep your counsels, never wrong'd you;
320   Save that, in love unto Demetrius,
        I told him of your stealth[77] unto this wood.
        He followed you; for love I followed him;
        But he hath chid me hence, and threatened me
        To strike me, spurn me, nay, to kill me too;
325   And now, so[78] you will let me quiet go,
        To Athens will I bear my folly back,
        And follow you no further. Let me go.
        You see how simple and how fond[79] I am.
HERMIA: Why, get you gone! Who is't that hinders you?
330 HELENA: A foolish heart that I leave here behind.
HERMIA: What! with Lysander?
HELENA: With Demetrius.
LYSANDER: Be not afraid; she shall not harm thee, Helena.
DEMETRIUS: No, sir, she shall not, though you take her part.
335 HELENA: O, when she is angry, she is keen and shrewd;
        She was a vixen when she went to school;
        And, though she be but little, she is fierce.
HERMIA: 'Little' again! Nothing but 'low' and 'little'!

[71]*wearing excessive makeup*

[72]*a tall, thin person*

[73]*argumentative*

[74]*being ill-tempered*

[75]*proper*

[76]*somewhat*

[77]*sneaking*

[78]*if*

[79]*foolish*

Why will you suffer her to flout me thus?

340   Let me come to her.

LYSANDER: Get you gone, you dwarf;

     You minimus, of hind'ring knot-grass[80†] made;

     You bead, you acorn.

DEMETRIUS: You are too officious[81]

345   In her behalf that scorns your services.

     Let her alone; speak not of Helena;

     Take not her part; for if thou dost intend

     Never so little show of love to her,

     Thou shalt aby[82] it.

350   LYSANDER: Now she holds me not.

     Now follow, if thou darest, to try whose right,

     Of thine or mine, is most in Helena.

DEMETRIUS: Follow! Nay, I'll go with thee, cheek by jowl.

                   Exeunt Lysander and Demetrius

HERMIA: You, mistress, all this coil[83] is 'long[84] of you.

355   Nay, go not back.

HELENA: I will not trust you, I;

     Nor longer stay in your curst company.

     Your hands than mine are quicker for a fray;[85]

     My legs are longer though, to run away.   *[Exit]*

360   HERMIA: I am amazed, and know not what to say.   *Exit*

OBERON: This is thy negligence. Still thou mistakest,

     Or else committ'st thy knaveries wilfully.

PUCK: Believe me, king of shadows, I mistook.

     Did not you tell me I should know the man

365   By the Athenian garments he had on?

     And so far blameless proves my enterprise,

     That I have 'nointed an Athenian's eyes;

     And so far am I glad it so did sort,

     As this their jangling[86] I esteem a sport.

370   OBERON: Thou seest these lovers seek a place to fight.

     Hie[87] therefore, Robin, overcast the night;

     The starry welkin[88] cover thou anon

     With drooping fog as black as Acheron,[†]

     And lead these testy rivals so astray

375   As one come not within another's way.

     Like to Lysander sometime frame thy tongue,

     Then stir Demetrius up with bitter wrong;

[80]*weeds*

[81]*meddlesome*

[82]*pay for*

[83]*turmoil*

[84]*because*

[85]*fight*

[86]*bickering*

[87]*Hurry*

[88]*sky*

And sometime rail thou like Demetrius;
And from each other look thou lead them thus,
380   Till o'er their brows death-counterfeiting sleep
With leaden legs and batty[89] wings doth creep.
Then crush this herb into Lysander's eye;
Whose liquor hath this virtuous[90] property,
To take from thence all error with his might
385   And make his eyeballs roll with wonted[91] sight.
When they next wake, all this derision
Shall seem a dream and fruitless vision;
And back to Athens shall the lovers wend,[92]
With league[93] whose date[94] till death shall never end.
390   Whiles I in this affair do thee employ,
I'll to my queen, and beg her Indian boy;
And then I will her charmed eye release
From monster's view, and all things shall be peace.
PUCK: My fairy lord, this must be done with haste,
395   For night's swift dragons† cut the clouds full fast;
And yonder shines Aurora's harbinger,†
At whose approach, ghosts, wandering here and there,
Troop home to churchyards. Damned spirits all
That in crossways[95]† and floods have burial,
400   Already to their wormy beds are gone,
For fear lest day should look their shames upon;
They wilfully themselves exile from light,
And must for aye[96] consort with black-brow'd night.
OBERON: But we are spirits of another sort:
405   I with the morning's love have oft made sport;
And, like a forester, the groves may tread
Even till the eastern gate, all fiery-red,
Opening on Neptune† with fair blessed beams,
Turns into yellow gold his salt green streams.
410   But, notwithstanding, haste, make no delay;
We may effect this business yet ere day.   *[Exit Oberon]*
PUCK: Up and down, up and down,
I will lead them up and down.
I am fear'd in field and town.
415   Goblin,[97] lead them up and down.
Here comes one.

[89]*bat-like*

[90]*potent*

[91]*normal*

[92]*go*

[93]*a covenant;*
   promise

[94]*duration*

[95]*crossroads*

[96]*forever*

[97]*Puck (addressing*
   himself)

Enter Lysander [Lysander and Demetrius wander on stage as if in the dark.]

LYSANDER: Where art thou, proud Demetrius? Speak thou now.

98 *with sword drawn*

PUCK: Here, villain, drawn[98] and ready. Where art thou?

99 *immediately*

LYSANDER: I will be with thee straight.[99]

420 PUCK: Follow me, then,
    To plainer[100] ground.

100 *smoother*

Enter Demetrius

DEMETRIUS: Lysander, speak again.
    Thou runaway, thou coward, art thou fled?
    Speak! In some bush? Where dost thou hide thy head?
PUCK: Thou coward, art thou bragging to the stars,
425   Telling the bushes that thou look'st for wars,

101 *coward*

    And wilt not come? Come, recreant,[101] come, thou child;
    I'll whip thee with a rod. He is defiled
    That draws a sword on thee.
DEMETRIUS: Yea, art thou there?
430 PUCK: Follow my voice; we'll try no manhood here.

                      [Exeunt]

[Re-enter Lysander]

LYSANDER: He goes before me, and still dares me on;
    When I come where he calls, then he is gone.
    The villain is much lighter-heel'd than I.
    I followed fast, but faster he did fly,   *Shifting places*
435   That fallen am I in dark uneven way,
    And here will rest me. Come, thou gentle day.

                      Lie[s] down

    For if but once thou show me thy grey light,
    I'll find Demetrius, and revenge this spite.

                      [Sleeps]

[Re]-enter [Puck] and Demetrius

102 *Wait for*

PUCK: Ho, ho, ho! Coward, why com'st thou not?

103 *know*

440 DEMETRIUS: Abide[102] me, if thou darest; for well I wot[103]

Thou runnest before me, shifting every place,
And darest not stand, nor look me in the face.
Where art thou now?
PUCK: Come hither; I am here.
445 DEMETRIUS: Nay, then, thou mock'st me. Thou shalt buy this
          dear,[104]   [104]*pay dearly*
     If ever I thy face by daylight see;
     Now, go thy way. Faintness constraineth me
     To measure out my length on this cold bed.
450 By day's approach look to be visited.
                              [Lies down and sleeps]

Enter Helena

HELENA: O weary night, O long and tedious night,
     Abate[105] thy hours! Shine comforts from the east,   [105]*Shorten*
     That I may back to Athens by daylight,
     From these that my poor company detest.
455 And sleep, that sometimes shuts up sorrow's eye,
     Steal me awhile from mine own company.
                              [Lies down and] sleep[s]
PUCK: Yet but three? Come one more;
     Two of both kinds makes up four.
     Here she comes, curst[106] and sad.   [106]*angry*
460 Cupid is a knavish lad,
     Thus to make poor females mad.

Enter Hermia

HERMIA: Never so weary, never so in woe,
     Bedabbled[107] with the dew, and torn with briers,   [107]*Sprinkled*
     I can no further crawl, no further go;
465 My legs can keep no pace with my desires.
     Here will I rest me till the break of day.
     Heavens shield Lysander, if they mean a fray!
                              [Lies down and sleeps]
PUCK: On the ground
                  Sleep sound;
470   I'll apply
                  To your eye,

Gentle lover, remedy.
> *[Squeezing the juice on Lysander's eyes]*
When thou wakest,
Thou takest
475   True delight
In the sight
Of thy former lady's eye;
And the country proverb known,
That every man should take his own,
480   In your waking shall be shown:
Jack shall have Jill;
Nought shall go ill;
The man shall have his mare again, and all shall be well.

[Exit]

ACT IV

A MIDSUMMER NIGHT'S DREAM

ACT IV

SCENE I
[The wood. Lysander, Demetrius,
Helena, and Hermia, lying asleep]

*Enter [Titania and Bottom; Peaseblossom, Cobweb, Moth,
Mustardseed, and] Fairies [Oberon] behind them, [unseen]*

TITANIA: Come, sit thee down upon this flowery bed,
While I thy amiable¹ cheeks do coy,²
And stick musk-roses in thy sleek smooth head,
And kiss thy fair large ears, my gentle joy.

5 BOTTOM: Where's Peaseblossom?

PEASEBLOSSOM: Ready.

BOTTOM: Scratch my head, Peaseblossom. Where's Monsieur
Cobweb?

COBWEB: Ready.

10 BOTTOM: Monsieur Cobweb; good monsieur, get you your
weapons in your hand and kill me a red-hipped humble-
bee on the top of a thistle; and, good monsieur, bring
me the honey-bag. Do not fret yourself too much in the
action, monsieur; and, good monsieur, have a care the

15 honey-bag break not; I would be loth to have you over-
flown³ with a honey-bag, signior. Where's Monsieur
Mustardseed?

MUSTARDSEED: Ready.

BOTTOM: Give me your neaf,⁴ Monsieur Mustardseed. Pray

20 you, leave your courtesy, good monsieur.

MUSTARDSEED: What's your will?

BOTTOM: Nothing, good monsieur, but to help Cavalery⁵
Cobweb to scratch. I must to the barber's, monsieur; for
methinks I am marvellous hairy about the face; and I

25 am such a tender ass, if my hair do but tickle me I must
scratch.

¹*lovable*

²*caress*

³*submerged*

⁴*fist*

⁵*Cavalier*

59

TITANIA: What, wilt thou hear some music, my sweet love?

BOTTOM: I have a reasonable good ear in music. Let's have
the tongs⁶ and the bones.⁷   *Rural music*

30 TITANIA: Or say, sweet love, what thou desirest to eat.

BOTTOM: Truly, a peck of provender;⁸ I could munch your
good dry oats. Methinks I have a great desire to a bottle⁹
of hay. Good hay, sweet hay, hath no fellow.¹⁰

TITANIA: I have a venturous fairy that shall seek

35   The squirrel's hoard, and fetch thee new nuts.

BOTTOM: I had rather have a handful or two of dried peas.
But, I pray you, let none of your people stir me; I have
an exposition¹¹ of sleep come upon me.

TITANIA: Sleep thou, and I will wind thee in my arms.

40   Fairies, be gone, and be all ways away.

                     [Exeunt Fairies]

     So doth the woodbine the sweet honeysuckle
     Gently entwist; the female ivy so
     Enrings the barky fingers of the elm.
     O, how I love thee! how I dote on thee!   *[They sleep]*

Enter [Puck]

45 OBERON: Welcome, good Robin. See'st thou this sweet
         sight?
     Her dotage¹² now I do begin to pity;
     For, meeting her of late behind the wood,
     Seeking sweet favors for this hateful fool,
     I did upbraid her and fall out with her.
50   For she his hairy temples then had rounded
     With coronet of fresh and fragrant flowers;
     And that same dew which sometime on the buds
     Was wont to swell, like round and orient¹³ pearls
     Stood now within the pretty flowerets' eyes,
55   Like tears, that did their own disgrace bewail.
     When I had at my pleasure taunted her,
     And she in mild terms begg'd my patience,
     I then did ask of her her changeling child;
     Which straight she gave me, and her fairy sent
60   To bear him to my bower in fairy land.
     And now I have the boy, I will undo

---

⁶*musical triangle*

⁷*pieces of bone used as a musical instrument*

⁸*hay*

⁹*bundle*

¹⁰*equal*

¹¹*"disposition"*

¹²*infatuation*

¹³*lustrous; bright like the sun in the East*

This hateful imperfection of her eyes.
And, gentle Puck, take this transformed scalp
From off the head of this Athenian swain,
65   That he awaking when the other do
May all to Athens back again repair,
And think no more of this night's accidents
But as the fierce vexation of a dream.
But first I will release the fairy queen.   *[Touching her eyes]*
70   Be as thou wast wont to be;
See as thou was wont to see.
Dian's bud o'er Cupid's flower†
Hath such force and blessed power.
Now, my Titania; wake you, my sweet queen.
75   TITANIA: My Oberon! What visions have I seen!
Methought I was enamour'd of an ass.
OBERON: There lies your love.
TITANIA: How came these things to pass?
O, how mine eyes do loathe his visage[14] now!
80   OBERON: Silence awhile. Robin, take off this head.
Titania, music call; and strike more dead
Than common sleep of all these five the sense.
TITANIA: Music, ho, music, such as charmeth sleep!   *[Music]*
PUCK: Now when thou wakest with thine own fool's eyes peep.
85   OBERON: Sound, music. Come, my Queen, take hands with me,
And rock the ground whereon these sleepers be.
Now thou and I are new in amity,[15]
And will tomorrow midnight solemnly
Dance in Duke Theseus' house triumphantly,
90   And bless it to all fair prosperity.
There shall the pairs of faithful lovers be
Wedded, with Theseus, all in jollity.
PUCK: Fairy king, attend and mark;
I do hear the morning lark.
95   OBERON: Then, my Queen, in silence sad,
Trip we after night's shade.
We the globe can compass[16] soon,
Swifter than the wandering moon.
TITANIA: Come, my lord; and in our flight,
100   Tell me how it came this night
That I sleeping here was found

[14]*face*

[15]*friendship*

[16]*orbit*

With these mortals on the ground.   *Exeunt*

Wind horns. Enter Theseus, Egeus, Hippolyta, and all his train

THESEUS: Go, one of you, find out the forester;
For now our observation† is perform'd,
And since we have the vaward[17] of the day,
My love shall hear the music of my hounds.
Uncouple in the western valley; let them go.
Dispatch, I say, and find the forester.
                                    [Exit an Attendant]
We will, fair queen, up to the mountain's top,
And mark the musical confusion
Of hounds and echo in conjunction.
HIPPOLYTA: I was with Hercules and Cadmus† once,
When in a wood of Crete† they bay'd[18] the bear
With hounds of Sparta;† never did I hear
Such gallant chiding,[19] for, besides the groves,
The skies, the fountains, every region near
Seem'd all one mutual cry. I never heard
So musical a discord, such sweet thunder.
THESEUS: My hounds are bred out of the Spartan kind,
So flew'd,[20] so sanded;[21] and their heads are hung
With ears that sweep away the morning dew;
Crook-knee'd and dew-lapp'd like Thessalian† bulls;
Slow in pursuit, but match'd in mouth like bells,
Each under each. A cry more tuneable
Was never holla'd to, nor cheer'd with horn,
In Crete, in Sparta, nor in Thessaly.
Judge when you hear. But, soft,[22] what nymphs are these?
EGEUS: My lord, this is my daughter here asleep,
And this Lysander, this Demetrius is,
This Helena, old Nedar's Helena.
I wonder of their being here together.
THESEUS: No doubt they rose up early to observe
The rite of May; and, hearing our intent,
Came here in grace of our solemnity.[23]
But speak, Egeus; is not this the day
That Hermia should give answer of her choice?
EGEUS: It is, my lord.

105
110
115
120
125
130
135

[17]*earliest part*

[18]*chased*

[19]*barking*

[20]*having large folds of flesh around the mouth*

[21]*sandy colored*

[22]*stop*

[23]*ceremony*

THESEUS: Go, bid the huntsmen wake them with their horns.
 Horns and they wake. Shouting within, the [lovers] all start up.
 Good-morrow, friends. Saint Valentine is past;†
140 Begin these wood-birds but to couple now?
LYSANDER: Pardon, my lord.
THESEUS: I pray you all, stand up.
 I know you two are rival enemies;
 How comes this gentle concord[24] in the world
145 That hatred is so far from jealousy
 To sleep by hate, and fear no enmity?[25]
LYSANDER: My lord, I shall reply amazedly,[26]
 Half sleep, half waking; but as yet, I swear,
 I cannot truly say how I came here,
150 But, as I think,—for truly would I speak,
 And now I do bethink me, so it is,—
 I came with Hermia hither. Our intent
 Was to be gone from Athens, where we might,
 Without[27] the peril of the Athenian law.
155 EGEUS: Enough, enough, my Lord; you have enough;
 I beg the law, the law upon his head.
 They would have stolen away, they would, Demetrius,
 Thereby to have defeated you and me:
 You of your wife, and me of my consent,
160 Of my consent that she should be your wife.
DEMETRIUS: My lord, fair Helen told me of their stealth,
 Of this their purpose hither to this wood;
 And I in fury hither followed them,
 Fair Helena in fancy following me.
165 But, my good lord, I wot not by what power,—
 But by some power it is,—my love to Hermia,
 Melted as the snow, seems to me now
 As the remembrance of an idle gaud[28]
 Which in my childhood I did dote upon;
170 And all the faith, the virtue of my heart,
 The object and the pleasure of mine eye,
 Is only Helena. To her, my lord,
 Was I betroth'd ere I saw Hermia.
 But, like a sickness, did I loathe this food;
175 But, as in health, come to my natural taste,

[24]*agreement*

[25]*hatred*

[26]*confusedly*

[27]*Beyond*

[28]*trinket*

Now I do wish it, love it, long for it,

And will for evermore be true to it.

THESEUS: Fair lovers, you are fortunately met;

Of this discourse we more will hear anon.

180   Egeus, I will overbear your will;

For in the temple, by and by, with us

These couples shall eternally be knit.

²⁹*because*

³⁰*somewhat*

And, for²⁹ the morning now is something³⁰ worn,

Our purposed hunting shall be set aside.

185   Away with us to Athens, three and three;

We'll hold a feast in great solemnity.

Come, Hippolyta.

Exeunt [Theseus, Hippolyta, Egeus, and train]

DEMETRIUS: These things seem small and undistinguishable,

Like far-off mountains turned into clouds.

³¹*unfocused*

190   HERMIA: Methinks I see these things with parted³¹ eye,

When every thing seems double.

HELENA: So methinks;

And I have found Demetrius like a jewel,

Mine own, and not mine own.

195   DEMETRIUS: Are you sure

That we are awake? It seems to me

That yet we sleep, we dream. Do not you think

The Duke was here, and bid us follow him?

HERMIA: Yea, and my father.

200   HELENA: And Hippolyta.

LYSANDER: And he did bid us follow to the temple.

DEMETRIUS: Why, then, we are awake; let's follow him;

And by the way let us recount our dreams.

Exeunt

BOTTOM: (*Wakes*) When my cue comes, call me, and I

205   will answer. My next is 'Most fair Pyramus.' Heigh-ho!

Peter Quince! Flute, the bellows-mender! Snout, the

tinker! Starveling! God's my life, stolen hence, and left

me asleep! I have had a most rare vision. I have had a

dream, past the wit of man to say what dream it was.

³²*tries*

210   Man is but an ass if he go about³² to expound³³ this

³³*explain*

dream. Methought I was—there is no man can tell what.

Methought I was, and methought I had, but man is but

³⁴*motley; like a jester or fool in motley clothes*

a patched³⁴ fool, if he will offer to say what methought I

215 had. The eye of man hath not heard, the ear of man hath
not seen, man's hand is not able to taste, his tongue to
conceive, nor his heart to report,† what my dream was.
I will get Peter Quince to write a ballad of this dream. It
shall be call'd 'Bottom's Dream,' because it hath no bottom; and I will sing it in the latter end of a play, before
220 the Duke. Peradventure,[35] to make it the more gracious, I
shall sing it at her death.

[35]*Perhaps*

Exit

SCENE II
[Athens.]

Enter Quince, [Flute], Snout, and Starveling

QUINCE: Have you sent to Bottom's house? Is he come home
   yet?
STARVELING: He cannot be heard of. Out of doubt he is trans-
   ported.
5 FLUTE: If he come not, then the play is marred; it goes not
   forward, doth it?
QUINCE: It is not possible. You have not a man in all Athens
   able to discharge[1] Pyramus but he.

[1]*play the part*

FLUTE: No; he hath simply the best wit of any handicraft man
10   in Athens.
QUINCE: Yea, and the best person[2] too; and he is a very paramour for a sweet voice.†

[2]*looks*

FLUTE: You must say 'paragon.'[3] A paramour[4] is—God bless
   us!—A thing of naught.

[3]*a model; a perfect*
[4]*adulterous lover*

Enter Snug the Joiner

15 SNUG: Masters, the Duke is coming from the temple; and
   there is two or three lords and ladies more married. If our
   sport had gone forward, we had all been made men.[5]
FLUTE: O sweet bully Bottom! Thus hath he lost sixpence
   a day during his life; he could not have scaped sixpence
20   a day. An the Duke had not given him sixpence a day

[5]*made our fortunes*

for playing Pyramus, I'll be hanged. He would have
deserved it: sixpence a day in Pyramus, or nothing.

Enter Bottom

BOTTOM: Where are these lads? Where are these hearts?
QUINCE: Bottom! O most courageous day! O most happy
25   hour!
BOTTOM: Masters, I am to discourse wonders; but ask me
not what; for if I tell you, I am not true Athenian. I will
tell you everything, right as it fell out.
QUINCE: Let us hear, sweet Bottom.
30 BOTTOM: Not a word of me. All that I will tell you is, that
the Duke hath dined. Get your apparel together; good
strings to your beards,[†] new ribbons to your pumps;[6]
meet presently at the palace; every man look o'er his
part; for the short and the long is, our play is preferred.
35   In any case, let Thisbe have clean linen; and let not him
that plays the lion pare[7] his nails, for they shall hang out
for the lion's claws. And, most dear actors, eat no onions
nor garlic, for we are to utter sweet breath; and I do not
doubt but to hear them say it is a sweet comedy. No
40   more words. Away, go, away!

Exeunt

[6]*men's shoes (often
decorated with
ribbons)*

[7]*trim*

ACT V

SCENE I
[Athens. The palace of Theseus]

Enter Theseus, Hippolyta, Philostrate, and Lords

HIPPOLYTA: 'Tis strange, my Theseus, that these lovers speak
    of.
THESEUS: More strange than true. I never may believe
    These antique fables, nor these fairy toys.[1]

5   Lovers and madmen have such seething[2] brains,
    Such shaping fantasies,[3] that apprehend[4]
    More than cool reason ever comprehends.
    The lunatic, the lover, and the poet,
    Are of imagination all compact.[5]

10   One sees more devils than vast hell can hold;
    That is the madman. The lover, all as frantic,
    Sees Helen's beauty† in a brow of Egypt.[6]
    The poet's eye, in a fine frenzy rolling,
    Doth glance from heaven to earth, from earth to heaven;

15   And as imagination bodies forth
    The forms of things unknown, the poet's pen
    Turns them to shapes, and gives to airy nothing
    A local habitation and a name.
    Such tricks hath strong imagination

20   That, if it would but apprehend some joy,
    It comprehends some bringer of that joy;
    Or in the night, imagining some fear,
    How easy is a bush supposed a bear?
HIPPOLYTA: But all the story of the night told over,

25   And all their minds transfigured so together,
    More witnesseth than fancy's images,[7]

[1]*tales*

[2]*boiling, frenzied*

[3]*imaginations*

[4]*conceive*

[5]*composed*

[6]*a gypsy's face*

[7]*"Shows that it was more than an illusion"*

67

And grows to something of great constancy,
But howsoever[8] strange and admirable.

Enter Lysander, Demetrius, Hermia, and Helena

THESEUS: Here come the lovers, full of joy and mirth.
30   Joy, gentle friends, joy and fresh days of love
         Accompany your hearts!
LYSANDER: More than to us
         Wait in your royal walks, your board, your bed!
THESEUS: Come now; what masques,[9] what dances shall
35   we have,
         To wear away this long age of three hours
         Between our after-supper and bed-time?
         Where is our usual manager of mirth?
         What revels are in hand? Is there no play
40   To ease the anguish of a torturing hour?
         Call Philostrate.
PHILOSTRATE: Here, mighty Theseus.
THESEUS: Say, what abridgment[10] have you for this evening?
         What masque? what music? How shall we beguile
45   The lazy time, if not with some delight?
PHILOSTRATE: There is a brief[11] how many sports[12] are ripe;[13]
         Make choice of which your Highness will see first.
                                   [Giving a paper]
THESEUS: 'The battle with the Centaurs,[†] to be sung
         By an Athenian eunuch[14] to the harp.'
50   We'll none of that: that have I told my love,
         In glory of my kinsman Hercules.[†]
         'The riot of the tipsy Bacchanals,[†]
         Tearing the Thracian singer in their rage.'
         That is an old device, and it was play'd
55   When I from Thebes came last a conqueror.
         'The thrice three Muses mourning for the death
         Of Learning, late deceas'd in beggary.'
         That is some satire, keen and critical,
         Not sorting with[15] a nuptial ceremony.
60   'A tedious brief scene of young Pyramus
         And his love Thisbe; very tragical mirth.'
         Merry and tragical! tedious and brief!

[8]*"in any case"*

[9]*entertaining activities*

[10]*entertainment*

[11]*list*

[12]*activities*

[13]*ready*

[14]*a castrated man (consequently having a high singing voice)*

[15]*appropriate for*

That is hot ice and wondrous strange snow.
How shall we find the concord of this discord?

65   PHILOSTRATE: A play there is, my lord, some ten words long,
        Which is as brief as I have known a play;
        But by ten words, my lord, it is too long,
        Which makes it tedious; for in all the play
        There is not one word apt, one player fitted.[16]   [16]*appropriately cast*
70   And tragical, my noble lord, it is;
        For Pyramus therein doth kill himself.
        Which when I saw rehearsed, I must confess,
        Made mine eyes water; but more merry tears
        The passion of loud laughter never shed.
75   THESEUS: What are they that do play it?
        PHILOSTRATE: Hard-handed men that work in Athens here,
        Which never labour'd in their minds till now;
        And now have toil'd[17] their unbreathed[18] memories   [17]*strained*
        With this same play against[19] your nuptial.   [18]*unpracticed*
                                                                                               [19]*in preparation for*
80   THESEUS: And we will hear it.
        PHILOSTRATE: No, my noble lord,
        It is not for you. I have heard it over,
        And it is nothing, nothing in the world;
        Unless you can find sport in their intents,
85   Extremely stretch'd and conn'd[20] with cruel pain,   [20]*memorized*
        To do you service.
        THESEUS: I will hear that play;
        For never anything can be amiss
        When simpleness and duty tender it.
90   Go, bring them in; and take your places, ladies.
                                                   [Exit Philostrate]
        HIPPOLYTA: I love not to see wretchedness[21] o'er-charged,[22]   [21]*lack of ability*
        And duty in his service perishing.   [22]*overburdened*
        THESEUS: Why, gentle sweet, you shall see no such thing.
        HIPPOLYTA: He says they can do nothing in this kind.
95   THESEUS: The kinder we, to give them thanks for nothing.
        Our sport shall be to take what they mistake;
        And what poor duty cannot do, noble respect
        Takes it in might, not merit.[†]
        Where I have come, great clerks[23] have purposed   [23]*scholars*
100 To greet me with premeditated welcomes;
        Where I have seen them shiver and look pale,

Make periods in the midst of sentences,
Throttle their practised accent in their fears,
And, in conclusion, dumbly have broke off,
105   Not paying me a welcome. Trust me, sweet,
Out of this silence yet I picked a welcome;
And in the modesty of fearful duty
I read as much as from the rattling tongue
Of saucy and audacious eloquence.
110   Love, therefore, and tongue-tied simplicity
In least speak most to my capacity.

[Re-enter Philostrate]

PHILOSTRATE: So please your Grace, the Prologue is
    address'd.²⁴
THESEUS: Let him approach.   *Flourish trumpets*

²⁴*ready*

Enter [Quince as] the Prologue

115 PROLOGUE: If we offend, it is with our good will.
    That you should think, we come not to offend,
    But with good will. To show our simple skill,
    That is the true beginning of our end.
    Consider then, we come but in despite.
120   We do not come, as minding²⁵ to content you,
    Our true intent is. All for your delight
    We are not here. That you should here repent you,
    The actors are at hand; and, by their show,
    You shall know all, that you are like to know.†

²⁵*intending*

125 THESEUS: This fellow doth not stand upon points.
LYSANDER: He hath rid his prologue like a rough²⁶ colt; he
    knows not the stop. A good moral, my lord: it is not
    enough to speak, but to speak true.
HIPPOLYTA: Indeed he hath play'd on this prologue like a
130   child on a recorder,––a sound, but not in government.²⁷
THESEUS: His speech was like a tangled chain; nothing
    impaired, but all disordered. Who is next?

²⁶*untamed*

²⁷*control*

Enter, with a trumpet before them, [as in dumb show,†] [Bottom
as] Pyramus and [Flute as] Thisbe, [Snout as] Wall, [Starveling
as] Moonshine, and [Snug as] Lion

PROLOGUE: Gentles, perchance you wonder at this show;
    But wonder on, till truth make all things plain.
135   This man is Pyramus, if you would know;
    This beauteous lady Thisbe is certain.
    This man, with lime and rough-cast, doth present
    Wall, that vile Wall which did these lovers sunder;[28]   [28]*separate*
    And through Wall's chink,[29] poor souls, they are content   [29]*crack, opening*
140   To whisper. At the which let no man wonder.
    This man, with lanthorn,[30] dog, and bush of thorn,   [30]*lantern*
    Presenteth Moonshine; for, if you will know,
    By moonshine did these lovers think no scorn
    To meet at Ninus' tomb,† there, there to woo.
145   This grisly beast, which Lion hight[31] by name,   [31]*is called*
    The trusty Thisbe, coming first by night,
    Did scare away, or rather did affright;
    And as she fled, her mantle[32] she did fall;   [32]*cloak*
    Which Lion vile with bloody mouth did stain.
150   Anon comes Pyramus, sweet youth and tall,[33]   [33]*brave*
    And finds his trusty Thisbe's mantle slain;
    Whereat with blade, with bloody blameful blade,
    He bravely broach'd[34] his boiling bloody breast;   [34]*stabbed*
    And Thisbe, tarrying in mulberry shade,
155   His dagger drew, and died. For all the rest,
    Let Lion, Moonshine, Wall, and lovers twain,[35]   [35]*two*
    At large discourse while here they do remain.
                      Exeunt all but Wall
THESEUS: I wonder if the lion be to speak.
DEMETRIUS: No wonder, my lord: one lion may, when many
160   asses do.
WALL: In this same interlude[36] it doth befall   [36]*play*
    That I, one Snout by name, present a wall;
    And such a wall as I would have you think
    That had in it a crannied hole or chink,
165   Through which the lovers, Pyramus and Thisbe,
    Did whisper often very secretly.
    This loam, this rough-cast, and this stone, doth show

37left (hand)

That I am that same wall; the truth is so;
And this the cranny is, right and sinister,37†
170   Through which the fearful lovers are to whisper.
THESEUS: Would you desire lime and hair to speak better?
DEMETRIUS: It is the wittiest partition that ever I heard dis-
    course, my lord.

Enter {Bottom as] Pyramus

THESEUS: Pyramus draws near the wall; silence.
175 PYRAMUS: O grim-look'd night! O night with hue so black!
    O night, which ever art when day is not!
    O night, O night, alack, alack, alack,
    I fear my Thisbe's promise is forgot!
    And thou, O wall, O sweet, O lovely wall,
180   That stand'st between her father's ground and mine;
    Thou wall, O wall, O sweet and lovely wall,
    Show me thy chink, to blink through with mine eyne.
    [Wall shows his chink]

38God reward you

    Thanks, courteous wall. Jove shield thee38 well for this!
    But what see I? No Thisbe do I see.
185   O wicked wall, through whom I see no bliss,
    Curs'd be thy stones for thus deceiving me!
THESEUS: The wall, methinks, being sensible, should curse

39back

    again.39
PYRAMUS: No, in truth, sir, he should not. Deceiving me is
190   Thisbe's cue. She is to enter now, and I am to spy her

40precisely

    through the wall. You shall see it will fall pat40 as I told
    you; yonder she comes.

Enter [Flute as] Thisbe

THISBE: O wall, full often hast thou heard my moans,
    For parting my fair Pyramus and me!
195   My cherry lips have often kiss'd thy stones,
    Thy stones with lime and hair knit up in thee.
PYRAMUS: I see a voice; now will I to the chink,
    To spy an I can hear my Thisbe's face.
    Thisbe!
200 THISBE: My love! thou art my love, I think.
PYRAMUS: Think what thou wilt, I am thy lover's grace;

And like Limander[41] am I trusty still.

THISBE: And I like Helen,[42] till the Fates me kill.

PYRAMUS: Not Shafalus to Procrus[43]† was so true.

205 THISBE: As Shafalus to Procrus, I to you.

PYRAMUS: O, kiss me through the hole of this vile wall.

THISBE: I kiss the wall's hole, not your lips at all.

PYRAMUS: Wilt thou at Ninny's[44] tomb meet me straightway?

THISBE: 'Tide life, 'tide death,[45] I come without delay.

210 WALL: Thus have I, wall, my part discharged so;

    And, being done, thus Wall away doth go.   *[Exeunt]*

THESEUS: Now is the mural down between the two neighbors.

DEMETRIUS: No remedy, my lord, when walls are so wilful to

    hear without warning.

215 HIPPOLYTA: This is the silliest stuff that ever I heard.

THESEUS: The best in this kind[46] are but shadows; and the

    worst are no worse, if imagination amend them.

HIPPOLYTA: It must be your imagination then, and not theirs.

THESEUS: If we imagine no worse of them than they of them-

220   selves, they may pass for excellent men. Here come two

    noble beasts in, a man and a lion.

Enter Lion and Moonshine

LION: You, ladies, you, whose gentle hearts do fear

    The smallest monstrous mouse that creeps on floor,

    May now, perchance, both quake and tremble here,

225   When lion rough in wildest rage doth roar.

    Then know that I, as Snug the joiner, am

    A lion fell,[47] nor else no lion's dam;[48]

    For, if I should as lion come in strife

    Into this place, 'twere pity on my life.

230 THESEUS: A very gentle beast, and of a good conscience.

DEMETRIUS: The very best at a beast, my lord, that e'er I saw.

LYSANDER: This lion is a very fox for his valour.

THESEUS: True; and a goose for his discretion.

DEMETRIUS: Not so, my lord; for his valour cannot carry his

235   discretion, and the fox carries the goose.

THESEUS: His discretion, I am sure, cannot carry his valour;

    for the goose carries not the fox. It is well. Leave it to his

    discretion, and let us listen to the moon.

MOONSHINE: This lanthorn doth the horned[49] moon present—

[41]*"Leander"*

[42]*Flute's mistake for "Hero"*

[43]*Bottom's mistake for "Cephalus and Procris"*

[44]*Ninus'*

[45]*"Come life or death"*

[46]*drama*

[47]*fierce*

[48]*mother*

[49]*crescent*

240 DEMETRIUS: He should have worn the horns on his head.

THESEUS: He is no crescent, and his horns are invisible
within the circumference.

MOONSHINE: This lanthorn doth the horned moon present;
Myself the man i' the moon do seem to be.

245 THESEUS: This is the greatest error of all the rest; the man
should be put into the lantern. How is it else the man i'
the moon?

DEMETRIUS: He dares not come there for the candle; for, you
see, it is already in snuff.[50]

250 HIPPOLYTA: I am aweary of this moon. Would he would
change!

THESEUS: It appears, by his small light of discretion, that
he is in the wane; but yet, in courtesy, in all reason, we
must stay the time.

255 LYSANDER: Proceed, Moon.

MOON: All that I have to say is to tell you that the lanthorn
is the moon; I, the man i' the moon; this thorn-bush, my
thorn-bush; and this dog, my dog.

DEMETRIUS: Why, all these should be in the lantern; for all
260   these are in the moon. But silence; here comes Thisbe.

[Re-]enter Thisbe

THISBE: This is old Ninny's tomb. Where is my love?

LION: O—   *The Lion roars [Flute as] Thisbe runs off*

DEMETRIUS: Well roared, Lion.

THESEUS: Well run, Thisbe.

265 HIPPOLYTA: Well shone, Moon. Truly, the moon shines with
a good grace.

[The Lion tears Thisbe's mantle, and exits]

THESEUS: Well moused, Lion.

DEMETRIUS: And then came Pyramus.

LYSANDER: And so the lion vanished.

[Re-]enter [Bottom as] Pyramus

270 PYRAMUS: Sweet Moon, I thank thee for thy sunny beams;
I thank thee, Moon, for shining now so bright;
For, by thy gracious, golden, glittering gleams,

[50]*angry*

I trust to take of truest Thisbe sight.
　　But stay, O spite!
275　　But mark, poor knight,
What dreadful dole[51] is here!
　　Eyes, do you see?
　　How can it he?
O dainty duck! O dear!
280　　Thy mantle good,
　　What! stain'd with blood?
Approach, ye Furies fell.
　　O Fates!† come, come;
　　Cut thread and thrum;
285　　Quail,[52] crush, conclude, and quell.[53]

THESEUS: This passion, and the death of a dear friend, would
　　go near to make a man look sad.

HIPPOLYTA: Beshrew my heart, but I pity the man.

PYRAMUS: O wherefore, Nature, didst thou lions frame?[54]
290　　Since lion vile hath here deflower'd[55] my dear;
Which is—no, no—which was the fairest dame
　　That lived, that loved, that liked, that looked with cheer.
　　Come, tears, confound;
　　Out, sword, and wound
295　　The pap[56] of Pyramus;
　　Ay, that left pap,
　　Where heart doth hop.
Thus die I, thus, thus, thus.　　*[Stabs himself]*
　　Now am I dead,
300　　Now am I fled;
My soul is in the sky.
　　Tongue, lose thy light;
　　Moon, take thy flight.　　　　*[Exit Moonshine]*
Now die, die, die, die, die.　　　　*[Dies]*

305 DEMETRIUS: No die, but an ace, for him; for he is but one.

LYSANDER: Less than an ace, man; for he is dead; he is
　　nothing.

THESEUS: With the help of a surgeon he might yet recover
　　and yet prove an ass.

310 HIPPOLYTA: How chance Moonshine is gone before Thisbe
　　comes back and finds her lover?

THESEUS: She will find him by starlight. Here she comes; and
　　her passion[57] ends the play.

[51]*sadness*

[52]*Overpower*

[53]*kill*

[54]*invent*

[55]*"devoured"*

[56]*breast*

[57]*speech*

[Re-]enter [Flute as] Thisbe]

HIPPOLYTA: Methinks she should not use a long one for
315   such a Pyramus; I hope she will be brief.
DEMETRIUS: A mote[58] will turn the balance, which Pyramus,
    which Thisbe, is the better,—he for a man, God warrant
    us: She for a woman, God bless us!
LYSANDER: She hath spied him already with those sweet
320   eyes.
DEMETRIUS: And thus she moans, videlicet:—
THISBE: Asleep, my love?
        What, dead, my dove?
    O Pyramus, arise,
325   Speak, speak. Quite dumb?
        Dead, dead? A tomb
    Must cover thy sweet eyes.
        These lily lips,
        This cherry nose,
330   These yellow cowslip cheeks,
        Are gone, are gone;
        Lovers, make moan;
    His eyes were green as leeks.
        O Sisters Three,†
335   Come, come to me,
    With hands as pale as milk;
        Lay them in gore,
        Since you have shore
    With shears his thread of silk.
340   Tongue, not a word.
        Come, trusty sword;
    Come, blade, my breast imbrue.[59]
                  [Stabs herself]
    And farewell, friends;
    Thus Thisbe ends;
345   Adieu, adieu, adieu.   *[Dies]*
THESEUS: Moonshine and Lion are left to bury the dead.
DEMETRIUS: Ay, and Wall too.
BOTTOM: No, I assure you; the wall is down that parted
    their fathers. Will it please you to see the epilogue, or to
350   hear a Bergomask dance† between two of our company?

[58]*speck*

[59]*make bloody*

THESEUS: No epilogue, I pray you; for your play needs no
       excuse. Never excuse; for when the players are all dead
       there need none to be blamed. Marry, if he that writ it had
       played Pyramus, and hanged himself in Thisbe's garter,
355   it would have been a fine tragedy. And so it is, truly; and
       very notably discharged. But come, your Bergomask; let
       your epilogue alone.   [*A dance*]
       The iron tongue of midnight hath told twelve.
       Lovers, to bed; 'tis almost fairy time.
360   I fear we shall out-sleep the coming morn,
       As much as we this night have overwatch'd.[60]
       This palpable[61]-gross[62] play hath well beguiled
       The heavy gait of night. Sweet friends, to bed.
       A fortnight[63] hold we this solemnity,
365   In nightly revels and new jollity.

                                                Exeunt

[60]*stayed up too late*

[61]*blatantly*

[62]*crude*

[63]*two weeks*

Enter Puck [with a broom]

PUCK: Now the hungry lion roars,
          And the wolf behowls the moon;
       Whilst the heavy ploughman snores,
          All with weary task fordone.[64]
370   Now the wasted brands[65] do glow,
          Whilst the screech-owl, screeching loud,
       Puts the wretch that lies in woe
          In remembrance of a shroud.
       Now it is the time of night
375   That the graves, all gaping wide,
       Every one lets forth his sprite,[66]
          In the church-way paths to glide.
       And we fairies, that do run
          By the triple Hecate's[†] team
380   From the presence of the sun,
          Following darkness like a dream,
       Now are frolic. Not a mouse
          Shall disturb this hallow'd house.
       I am sent with broom before,
385   To sweep the dust behind the door.

[64]*weary*

[65]*burned-out logs*

[66]*ghost*

Enter [Oberon and Titania], with all their train

OBERON: Through the house give glimmering light,
    By the dead and drowsy fire;
    Every elf and fairy sprite
      Hop as light as bird from brier;
390   And this ditty, after me,
    Sing and dance it trippingly.
TITANIA: First, rehearse your song by rote,
    To each word a warbling note;
    Hand in hand, with fairy grace,
395   Will we sing, and bless this place.

The Song

OBERON: Now, until the break of day,
    Through this house each fairy stray.
    To the best bride-bed will we,
    Which by us shall blessed be;
400   And the issue there create
    Ever shall be fortunate.
    So shall all the couples three
    Ever true in loving be;
    And the blots of Nature's hand
405   Shall not in their issue stand;
    Never mole, hare-lip, nor scar,
    Nor mark[67] prodigious,[68] such as are
    Despised in nativity,
    Shall upon their children be.
410   With this field-dew consecrate,[69]
    Every fairy take his gait,
    And each several[70] chamber bless,
    Through this palace, with sweet peace;
    And the owner of it blest
415   Ever shall in safety rest.
    Trip away; make no stay;
    Meet me all by break of day.   *Exeunt [all but Puck]*
PUCK: If we shadows have offended,
    Think but this, and all is mended,
420   That you have but slumber'd here

[67]*birthmark*

[68]*abnormal*

[69]*blessed dew*

[70]*separate*

While these visions did appear.
And this weak and idle theme,
No more yielding but a dream,
Gentles, do not reprehend.
425   If you pardon, we will mend.
And, as I am an honest Puck,
If we have unearned luck
Now to scape[71] the serpent's tongue,[72]
We will make amends ere long;
430   Else the Puck a liar call.
So, good night unto you all.
Give me your hands,[73] if we be friends,
And Robin shall restore amends.   *[Exit]*

[71]*escape*

[72]*hisses from the audience*

[73]*applaud*

THE END

GLOSSARY

Act I, Scene I

dowager – a widow who receives property from her deceased husband

"dream away the time" – This phrase foreshadows the following days' events and how they will be perceived as dreams.

Your Grace – addressing Theseus, the Duke of Athens

"...the ancient privilege...dispose of her..." – By Athenian law, a father had the authority to send his daughter to a convent or have her killed if she were to disobey him.

"the cold fruitless moon" – an allusion to Diana, the Roman goddess of chastity ("fruitless") and goddess of the moon

maiden pilgrimage – living life as a virgin

Diana – See note *the cold fruitless moon* above.

spotted – a person who is morally stained

leagues – Originally, a league was the unit of distance the average person could walk in one hour.

"To do observance to a morn of May" – "To celebrate May Day"; May Day marked the summer solstice (around June 21), which is when the sun reaches its northernmost point and marks the middle of summer (Midsummer).

"Cupid's strongest bow...golden head..." – Cupid (the Roman god of love) was often portrayed carrying a golden-tipped arrow.

Venus' doves – In Roman mythology, Venus (the goddess of love and beauty) traveled in a carriage drawn by doves.

"...by that fire...sail was seen..." – an allusion to Vergil's *Aeneid*, in which he describes Dido's love for Aeneas, a Trojan hero; when Aeneas sails away for Italy, Dido throws herself onto a burning funeral pyre.

Phoebe – a Titan in Greek mythology associated with the moon

"o'er other some" – "when compared to others"

Act I, Scene II

Quince – a pun on "quoins," wooden wedges used in carpentry

Snug – The name suggests well-fitted furniture.

Bottom – A "bottom" is a piece of wood on which thread is wound. "Bottom" also is a pun on "ass," which he becomes.

Starveling – Tailors during Shakespeare's time were stereotyped as being thin.

generally – Bottom mistakenly uses "generally" for "individually"; note that Bottom frequently misuses words in this fashion.

Phibbus – Phoebus Apollo, the Greek god of sun and light

Fates – In both Greek and Roman myth, the Fates controlled human destiny. Clotho, the spinner (Nona), was said to spin the thread of life. Lachesis (Decuma), the measurer, determined the length of one's life and one's lot in life. Atropos (Morta) had the duty of cutting the life thread when a person arrived at the end of his or her life.

"Nay, faith...beard coming." – In Elizabethan theater, men or young boys played female characters.

"Some of your...at all..." – a disease attributed to the French that resulted in hair loss

"hold, or cut bow-strings" – Cutting a bow's string renders it useless, so it might refer to military archers who, unable to hold a position, cut their own bow-strings to prevent the enemy from shooting the discarded weapons.

Act II, Scene I

Puck – a common name for an imp or devil

moon's sphere – A transparent sphere was thought to exist around the moon and each planet.

changeling – a child left in place of one stolen by fairies

Robin Goodfellow – a trickster figure of Elizabethan folklore

'tailor' – possibly an expression of pain from landing on her tailbone

Corin; Phillida – traditional names of shepherds and shepherdesses

Amazon – Hippolyta, in Greek mythology, was queen of the Amazons who led the attack on Athens.

Perigouna; Aegle – Theseus' mistresses

Ariadne – a heroine in Greek mythology who helped Theseus defeat the Minotaur

Antiopa – Hippolyta's sister

Neptune – the Greek god of the sea

watery moon – The moon was often associated with water because it controlled the tides.

"Apollo flies...the chase" – a reversal of the myth in which Daphne flees from Apollo and is turned into a laurel tree to escape his clutches

griffin – a mythical creature with a lion's body and an eagle's head and wings

Act II, Scene II

Newts and blind-worms – Both newts and blindworms (small, limbless lizards) were thought to be poisonous.

Philomel – a nightingale; in mythology, Philomel was transformed into a nightingale after being raped by her brother-in-law.

"...take the sense, sweet, of my innocence!" – "...understand, dear, my noble intentions!"

"...Or as the heresies...they did deceive..." – "Men usually regret the opinions they once believed"; Lysander used to dislike Helena. Now he's trying to convince her that his feelings are genuine by admitting to being wrong.

Act III, Scene I

"written in eight and six" – a standard ballad meter (alternating lines of eight and six syllables)

a bush of thorns – In folklore, the man in the moon carried a bundle of kindling.

Jew – Flute is punning on juvenal; referring to someone as a Jew was derogatory and not considered lovely at all.

Ninus – the founder of Nineveh, the setting of Pyramus and Thisbe

a fire – a reference to a phenomenon known as *ignis fatuus*, or *will-o'-the-wisp*, usually seen in fields at night as a type of light

"You see an ass-head...own..." – "You see a figment of your own imagination..."

"dares not answer nay..." – "dares not deny"; the cuckoo's song was said to mock cuckolds, or men whose wives were unfaithful.

"If I cut my finger..." – Cobwebs were oftentimes used to stop bleeding.

weeps every little flower – The moon was thought to produce dew.

Act III, Scene II

"...and so displease / Her brothers..." – Apollo, the sun god (brother of Diana, the moon goddess)

"the moon / May...the Antipodes." – *Antipodes* referred to anyone who lived on the other side of the world. Essentially, Hermia is saying that it is impossible to believe that Lysander left her; she would sooner believe that there was a hole in the earth that reached through to the other side, disturbed the Antipodes, and filled their world with sunlight when it should have been dark.

Tartar – a term Europeans used when referring to individuals from Asian tribes; Tartars were known for their archery skills.

"badge of faith" – Lysander's figurative badge is his tears.

Taurus – a mountain range in present-day Turkey

Ethiope – This insult is directed specifically at Hermia's dark hair and complexion.

"...you puppet..." – Hermia interprets the use of "puppet" as an attack on her height.

hind'ring knot-grass – This creeping weed's sap was believed to stunt a person's growth.

Acheron – a river in Hades, specifically, the river of woe

night's swift dragons – Nyx, the goddess of night in Greek mythology was believed to have dragons drawing her chariot.

Aurora's harbinger – Aurora's messenger; Aurora is the goddess of the dawn, and her messenger would be Venus, the morning star.

crossways – where suicides were buried

Act IV, Scene I

"Dian's bud o'er Cupid's flower" – Oberon is removing the spell ("Cupid's flower") from Titania's eyes; the antidote Oberon is using, "Dian's bud," is named for Diana, goddess of chastity.

observation – referring to the observance of May Day

Cadmus – a Phoenician prince in Greek mythology, who founded the city of Thebes

Crete – a Greek island

hounds of Sparta – dogs famous for their hunting skills

Thessalian – referring to a region in Greece known as Thessaly

"Saint Valentine is past" – It was believed that birds chose their mates on St. Valentine's Day, just as Hermia is to choose hers on this day.

"The eye of man...heart to report..." – Bottom, as usual, has confused his words. In this instance, Bottom has confused the biblical verse from Corinthians 2:9, which reads, "The eye hath not seen, and the ear hath not heard, neither have entered into the heart of man...."

Act IV, Scene II

"…he is a very paramour…sweet voice." – Quince does not know or understand the word "paramour"; his mistake is corrected by Flute in his response.

"strings to your beards" – referring to the strings attached to beards used in costumes

Act V, Scene I

Helen's beauty – Helen of Troy was considered to have been the most beautiful woman in the world.

" 'The battle…Centaurs…' " – one of Hercules' famous battles

"…my kinsman Hercules." – In mythology, Hercules and Theseus were cousins.

" 'The riot…Bacchanals…' " – a reference to an ancient Roman festival, during which riotous, drunken women of Thrace (a country in southeast Europe) dismembered the poet Orpheus with their bare hands

"noble respect…not merit." – Theseus is saying that he considers the effort, not the quality of the product: ("It's the thought that counts").

"If we offend…like to know." – Quince's faulty interpretation distorts the meaning of the prologue.

as in dumb show – A "dumb show" is a show before or after a production in which actors introduce their characters or silently dramatize a narrator's monologue.

Ninus' tomb – See note *Ninus* in Act III, Scene I.

"right and sinister" – Snout uses his hands to simulate the cranny.

Limander – Bottom mistakenly refers to Leander as Limander; Leander was a fabled lover who drowned while swimming to meet Hero, his lover.

"Shafalus to Procurus" – tragic lovers

Fates – See note *Fates* in Act I, Scene II.

Sisters Three – another reference to the Fates

Bergomask dance – a rustic dance named for Bergamo, Italy

Hecate – In Greek mythology, Hecate was the goddess of magic and spells. She is identified with three other goddesses: Selene (Luna), goddess of the moon, Artemis (Diana), goddess of virginity, hunting, and the moon; and Persephone (Proserpina), queen of the underworld (Hades). Because of Hecate's association with these goddesses, she is usually depicted as having three bodies and three heads so she can see in all directions.

VOCABULARY

Act I, Scene I
abjure – to give up, reject
aught – anything
avouch – to declare
beguiled – deceived
beseech – to beg, plead
brake – an area overgrown with plants; a thicket
dotes – idolizes, worships
edict – a law; a declaration
enthrall'd – enslaved (by love)
entreat – to ask, beg
ere – before
mirth – merriment, laughter
pale – colorless
perjured – forsworn; lying under oath
siege – to attack; to gain entrance (used metaphorically in this context)
trifles – small gifts; sweets
vexation – aggravation; turmoil
vile – disgusting
visage – a face

Act I, Scene II
bellows – a chamber used to pump air onto a fire to keep it ablaze
dogg'd – bothered
discretion – consideration; judgment
interlude – a short play (usually performed between the acts of a longer play)
lofty – impressive, sublime
mar – to harm, injure
marry – an oath expressing surprise or emphasis
tawny – tan in color

Act II, Scene I
brier – a type of plant with thorny or prickly stems
chaste – pure
chide – to reprimand (also seen as *chid*)
crimson – red in color
dale – a valley
dissension – a disagreement
flout – to scorn
forsooth – indeed
rear – to raise or bring up
woodbine – a type of plant similar to honeysuckle

Act II, Scene II
clamorous – noisy
disdainful – hateful
dissembling – deceitful
flout – to flaunt; expose
heresies – controversial opinions (usually considered to be false)
swoon – to faint

Act III, Scene I
abide – to bear, tolerate, put up with
auditor – an audience member
bower – an arbor; a woman's chamber in a castle; a cottage
brake – an area overgrown with plants; a thicket
knavery – mischief; trickery
loam – a mixture of clay, sand, and straw
parlous – [*perilous*] risky, dangerous
rough-cast – a mixture of lime and gravel

Act III, Scene II
asunder – split into pieces
chronicled – recorded
confederacy – a group of people united to commit an unlawful act; a conspiracy
confounding – confusing; mixing up
congealed – solidified; frozen
cur – a dog; a coward
derision – ridicule
disparage – to mock, belittle
forester – the official responsible for the forest land
fray – a fight
heraldry – the system used for creating different symbols or shields to identify specific families
minimus – [Latin] of the smallest size
preposterously – foolishly, absurdly
vixen – an ill-tempered woman

Act IV, Scene I
coronet – a small crown, garland, or wreath
discord – disharmony
peck – a quarter bushel (8 quarts)
swain – a man who dates a woman; a suitor
upbraid – to scold, reprimand

Act IV, Scene II
marred – ruined

<u>Act V, Scene I</u>
hare-lip – a congenital cleft in the center of the upper lip
tarrying – waiting
thrum – the leftover tufts of yarn on a loom
videlicet – as follows
wane – declining gradually

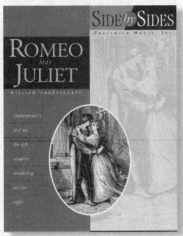

Insightful and Reader-Friendly, Yet Affordable

Prestwick House Literary Touchstone Classic Editions–
The Editions By Which All Others May Be Judged

Every *Prestwick House Literary Touchstone Classic* is enhanced with Reading Pointers for Sharper Insight to improve comprehension and provide insights that will help students recognize key themes, symbols, and plot complexities. In addition, each title includes a Glossary of the more difficult words and concepts.

For the Shakespeare titles, along with the Reading Pointers and Glossary, we include margin notes and various strategies to understanding the language of Shakespeare.

New titles are constantly being added; call or visit our website for current listing.

Special Educator's Discount – At Least
50% Off

		Retail Price	Educator's Discount
200053	**Adventures of Huckleberry Finn**	$4.99	**$2.49**
202118	**Antigone**	$3.99	**$1.99**
200141	**Awakening, The**	$5.99	**$2.99**
200179	**Christmas Carol, A**	$3.99	**$1.99**
200694	**Doll's House, A**	$3.99	**$1.99**
200054	**Frankenstein**	$4.99	**$1.99**
200091	**Hamlet**	$3.99	**$1.99**
200074	**Heart of Darkness**	$3.99	**$1.99**
200147	**Importance of Being Earnest, The**	$3.99	**$1.99**
200146	**Julius Caesar**	$3.99	**$1.99**
200125	**Macbeth**	$3.99	**$1.99**
200081	**Midsummer Night's Dream, A**	$3.99	**$1.99**
200079	**Narrative of the Life of Frederick Douglass**	$3.99	**$1.99**
200564	**Oedipus Rex**	$3.99	**$1.99**
200095	**Othello**	$3.99	**$1.99**
200193	**Romeo and Juliet**	$3.99	**$0.99**
200132	**Scarlet Letter, The**	$5.99	**$2.99**
200251	**Tale of Two Cities, A**	$6.99	**$3.49**

P:Prestwick House

Prestwick House, Inc. • P.O. Box 658, Clayton, DE 19938
Phone (800) 932-4593 • Fax (888) 718-9333 • www.prestwickhouse.com